EMMANUEL KOLINI

EMMANUEL KOLINI

THE UNLIKELY ARCHBISHOP OF RWANDA

MARY WEEKS MILLARD

COLORADO SPRINGS · MILTON KEYNES · HYDERABAD

Authentic Publishing
We welcome your questions and comments.

USA   1820 Jet Stream Drive, Colorado Springs, CO 80921
          www.authenticbooks.com
UK   9 Holdom Avenue, Bletchley, Milton Keynes, Bucks, MK1 1QR
          www.authenticmedia.co.uk
India   Logos Bhavan, Medchal Road, Jeedimetla Village, Secunderabad
          500 055, A.P.

Emmanuel Kolini
ISBN 13: 9781934068656

Copyright © 2008 by Mary Weeks Millard

10 09 08 / 6 5 4 3 2 1

Published in 2008 by Authentic
A catalog record for this book is available through the Library of Congress.

Cover and interior design: projectluz.com
Editorial team: Bette Smyth, Karen James, Dan Johnson, Michaela Dodd

Printed in the United States of America

Dedication

I would like to dedicate this book to Alison Joy Weeks, my little daughter, whose body lies buried in the Congo, but whose spirit is with the risen Lord, and to all the children who perished in 1994 during the genocide in Rwanda.

— *Mary Weeks Millard*
Weymouth, England
March 2008

~~~~~~

To all those who have contributed significantly to our walk with Christ:

Late Erasto Abisagi Kato (Uganda)
Late Tito and Mrs. Dorootyo
Rev. E. Obaya
Rev. Vuningoma (Rwanda)

Rev. Yona Kanamuzeyi (Rwanda)

Ven. S. Nyarubona

Bishop Festo Kivengere

Bishop Yustasi Ruhindi

Bishop Yonathan Rwakaikara

Msgr. Aloys Bigirumwami (Rwanda)

Archbishop Bezareli Ndahura (Congo)

Archbishop Eric Sabiiti

Eric Wood (Zimbabwe)

Raymond, Brethren missionary from New Zealand

Yonas and Esther Majara (Uganda)

Mfakati Kwanya Atenyi (Uganda)

John and Mrs. Hayward (England)

Also for all those who have loved and died for justice, and for all those who have served as peacemakers.

— *Emmanuel and Freda Kolini*

Foreword

In the biblical record of the life of the early church, we discover this generous and unassuming missionary leader whom the apostles nicknamed Barnabas, meaning "Son of Encouragement" (Acts 4:36). He was called such because of the tremendous hope and encouragement that he kept bringing to the church of his day as it moved through its many difficulties, challenges, and opportunities. Described simply as "a good man, full of the Holy Spirit and faith" (Acts 11:24), this bold and prophetic leader not only walked closely with those earliest apostles, but also walked closely with God.

In the pages of the book you are now holding, you will discover and read with fascination the story of another man who walks closely with God: a quiet and unassuming missionary leader who is being used powerfully by God to bring hope and encouragement to the church of the twenty-first century. Your faith will be strengthened, your world expanded, and your heart truly stirred by this amazing story of a remarkable man of God.

— *The Right Reverend Chuck Murphy*
Chairman of the Anglican Mission
in the Americas (AMiA)

Rwanda

O Africa, cradled within your heart
Lies a place which has wound itself round mine,
Rwanda, a jewel, you stand apart,
"Land of a thousand hills" with views sublime.

Yet you shelter within your valleys there
Your weeping children, burdened with their pain;
Dark hillsides absorbing the secrets, where
Slaughter and murder have left bloody stain.

In serenity the banana grows
Silent witness to your fertility
While in the byre the newborn calf now lows;
Life has regained some normality.

So, brother, in forgiveness, let there be peace,
May love return, and hostilities cease.

— *Mary Weeks Millard*
2007

CONTENTS

Introduction

One day in 2006 I was sitting with Archbishop Emmanuel Musaba Kolini in his diocesan office in Kigali. We were having a cup of tea and discussing a book I had written about a young man in Uganda. Laughingly, he said to me, "It's my story you should be writing!"

I laughed with him, answering, "Yes, maybe someday!" not thinking for one minute that he was serious about what he said. However, the seed was planted in my mind. Later that year I returned to Rwanda, taking some friends with me. It was the time of the national mourning week, beginning on April 7, a poignant time of remembrance for the Rwandese people.[1] Once again I found myself sitting and talking with Archbishop Kolini, this time about one of his priests whose story I was about to write. "It's my story you should be writing!" the archbishop said to me.

This time I didn't laugh it off because I realized that Kolini was serious. I promised that when he felt the time was right I would be willing to help him. We agreed to work together on the project, because as Kolini nears the end of his ecclesiastical career, we realize that his story and that of his wife, Freda Mukakarinda, could bless and encourage many.

I believe this book has been in the purposes of God for many years. Even while Emmanuel Kolini was living as a refugee in Uganda, the Lord began speaking to him in French, giving him the theme for a book he would one day share with the world. French was the language of the Catholic Church at that time that he was most familiar with. The title was *Le Seigneur Fut pour Moi des Choses Merveilleux* (*The Lord Has Done Wonderful Things for Me*). As I sat with Kolini and heard his story, my spirit rose—"Amen!" Listening to his testimony has thrilled my heart. Like Mary the mother of Jesus singing praise to the Lord in the words of the Magnificat, Archbishop Kolini echoes those same words of praise to God for all his goodness to him throughout his life.

All of us who have lived through the last half of the twentieth and the first part of the twenty-first centuries have experienced very turbulent times. Most countries of the world have been affected by wars, terrorism, natural disasters, and increasingly pressurized living conditions, quickened by huge advances in science and technology. Our lives have seen so many changes in a short span of time. These changes have brought increasing anxiety, so the emotional health of many is suffering. Drug companies have benefited from this ever-growing need for people to find peace through tranquilizers, in order to make it through the day.

For other people, however, these same challenges have been the fire that has forged them into the people they are now: leaders able to inspire many. Such leaders are much needed in this day and age, willing to stand out from the crowd, make their voices heard, and inspire and encourage us to move forward.

When I was just beginning to think about writing this book, I read Joel 1:1–20 for my morning Bible study. Scripture Union's *Encounter with God* [2] had this comment on these verses, quoted with permission: "Consider earthquakes and hurricanes, tsunami, wars and invasions, terrorist attacks, bird flu. . . . For some readers these may have been terrible personal experiences; for most of us, perhaps, disturbing but distant events. The task of the faithful prophet is to signal God's faithful presence and purposes through all of life's events."

For many of us, the Rwandan genocide and the trauma that flowed from it were a disturbing but distant event, but for those living in Rwanda in 1994 and the years that followed, it has been a terrible personal experience. However, God called Kolini to be a prophet, along with many others, and he has been faithful in his ministry to both church and nation.

The purpose of this book is to tell the life story of one man, a prophet and leader, though not only his story and that of his wife, Freda, but also the story of his beloved country of Rwanda, many other people throughout Africa, and the Anglican Communion. [3]

I first met His Grace, Archbishop Emmanuel Kolini, in 2001. I was on a visit to Rwanda, along with a few other people from Great Britain, sent by a Christian charity, Signpost International, to see what help the organization might be able to give to some of the survivors of the 1994 genocide. At that time, although the genocide had occurred seven years before, the aftermath was still generating many humanitarian and spiritual needs. The archbishop welcomed our group both to the province of Rwanda and to the diocese of Kigali, where he presides as bishop.[4]

I immediately warmed to this gracious man, and as he addressed us, I sensed God's love. His smile lit up his whole face and embraced us. Here was a man who clearly cared deeply for his people and wanted to help them as a shepherd. He loved the youngest child and the poorest widow as well as the priests for whom he was responsible. On that first visit to Rwanda I also had the privilege of meeting his lovely wife, Freda, and since then have appreciated the friendship of this gentle woman of God who is such a fitting help to her husband.

Over the years our friendship has grown, and I have had the joy of returning many times to Rwanda, the beautiful "land of a thousand hills," as this jewel in the crown of Africa is affectionately known. So for me personally, it is a great joy and a huge privilege to be able to tell the stories of Archbishop Emmanuel Kolini and his wife, Freda.

I have also had the tremendous privilege of living and working in Uganda and Congo and, in more recent years, of frequently visiting Rwanda. I have a great love for these countries and the people who have suffered so much. The joy of the Christians, despite all their problems, never ceases to inspire me. As I have written these stories in previous books, in my imagination I have been transported back to these countries, so I hope that as you also read them, I am able to take you with me to help you understand, at least in some small degree, what Kolini and this part of Africa have gone through.

Everyone in a senior position of leadership within any organization will have to make decisions that can be difficult and controversial, and inevitably, some people are bound to disagree. This has certainly been the case for Archbishop Kolini. Though despite receiving such criticism and misunderstanding from both within the Anglican Church and outside it, he has, like the Pilgrim Fathers of old, been unswerving in his stand for biblical truth and Christian doctrine.

As I have learned more of his story, it has only increased my admiration and respect for this humble servant of God. My prayer is that as I share the stories of Kolini and Freda in this book, you will also be inspired and encouraged in your own personal journey with God.

— *Mary Weeks Millard*
Weymouth, England
Summer 2008

CHAPTER 1

Early Days

Kolini's life began in the year of the great famine called *Ruzagayura* that ravaged Rwanda and eastern Congo. As was often the case in Africa, the actual date of his birth was not recorded, though because of the famine, his mother knew it was 1945. He was born in what was then known as the Belgian Congo in a small township called Nyamitaba in the Masisi district some fifty miles west of Goma, a town bordering Rwanda. Kolini's family traveled quite freely between the two countries, as did most families that lived in this area, because at this time the border was drawn through an area without regard to the people who lived there and, in the early days, passports were not needed.

Although Nyamitaba was just a small town, it boasted a Roman Catholic church with its parish school and a Seventh-day

Adventist church. His parents attended neither of the churches and instead followed African traditional religion, because at this time they were not yet Christians.

This baby boy was the first child born to the Tutsi family and was named Kolini, the African version of Colin. There was a man named Colin who was a European administrator for whom his parents worked, milking the cows for him, and as they were working for him around the time of their baby's birth, his mother choose this name for her son.

God's Protection

His mother was not happy when she learned she was pregnant, for she was still a young girl. In her anger she tried to terminate the pregnancy three times, but the Lord clearly had plans for this new life; her efforts failed and Kolini lived. This was to be the first of many times God would protect and preserve his life.

As a young child, Kolini was taken to a village in Rwanda near the border town of Gisenyi at the foot of the volcanoes. Here he lived with his maternal grandparents. It is very common in this part of Africa for a small child to be brought up by members of the extended family. His parents also moved to Rwanda to live in Ruhengeri, a town in the north of the country, though some distance from Gisenyi. Kolini's earliest memories come from this time, so he assumed his grandparents were his mother and father until one day when his real mother visited, bringing a new shirt for him. It was his first realization that his grandmother was not his mother and that he had parents who lived somewhere else.

In the north of Rwanda, as in Congo, there are nomadic Pygmy tribes that live mostly in the forests. They are skilled at many things, enabling them to survive in difficult and primitive conditions. In the 1940s medical care was scarce in countries like Rwanda and even if available was unaffordable for most people. So when Kolini became sick with pneumonia, his grandmother turned to the Pygmies for help for the small child. They had knowledge of herbs and had learned numerous treatments for sickness.

Though strange compared to Western ways of treating pneumonia, they took a horn from a goat and sliced off the top to make a hollow tube. This sharp end was inserted into the lung area of the baby over a leaf picked from an inbatobata bush known to have healing properties. Then the Pygmy sucked out the blood and infection. When it was believed that all the infection had been removed and only pure blood was flowing, the goat's horn fell off, and the wound was covered with more healing leaves from the bush. These leaves were bound on like a poultice. Though unorthodox, this treatment was successful, and the baby quickly recovered.

Little Kolini had been very ill, and without the Pygmies' help, he would have probably died. The Lord kept his hand on the young boy.

In this mountainous part of northern Rwanda the ground is very fertile from volcanic lava, and the climate is ideal for growing peas and potatoes. Young Kolini would help his grandmother in the fields. One day he was in a field picking peas with her when he saw a white man, a *muzungu,* for the very first time. The bearded man dressed in a long robe was a Catholic priest. The little boy was terrified and ran away, stumbling and falling. There would be countless other encounters with *wazungu*[1] throughout his life; Kolini would later develop lasting relationships with many of them, but this was his first impression of a white man.

Another event Kolini remembers from that time was when a tornado hit the town of Gisenyi. Mud houses with thatched grass roofs were very vulnerable, as they had only a thin stick frame with mud pressed into them to form the walls, covered with a dried grass roof. As was usually done, his grandmother was cooking on a fire near the hut, and when the strong winds came, the fire quickly became a hazard and spread, threatening to burn several houses nearby. Everyone ran quickly to put out the fire burning near his grandmother's house as the high winds swirled through the town.

Death of His Grandfather

One day people began to gather at his grandparents' home. Young Kolini realized something unusual was happening but did not know what. His grandfather had died that day, and all the people had come to pay their respects and attend the funeral rites.[2]

His grandfather's death changed their lives. His grandmother decided they needed to leave the village and go to live with his real parents. The only way to Ruhengeri was on foot, so they packed their things, and with their belongings on her head and a small child at her side, Grandmother led the way on the two-day journey to their new home. This was a very long and bewildering trip for young Kolini. In the space of a few days his whole life had changed dramatically.

Grandmother and grandson arrived at the home of Kolini's parents, a small house in the shadow of the Muhabura volcano, not far from the bamboo forests where gorillas roam. It was in a beautiful area, though damp and cold when the mists descended from the mountain volcanoes. In the rainy season the streams from the mountains swell, flowing swiftly down to the river. When Kolini started attending the local Roman Catholic primary school, he had to cross this river twice a day.

Kolini's father worked for a Belgian plantation owner. The volcanic ground provided fertile soil for growing peas, potatoes, and pyrethrum. Pyrethrum is a daisy plant, a variety of chrysanthemum from which a powerful insecticide is extracted. Although it is used much less now, it was a very popular crop during the 1960–1970s. The pollinating daisy heads are harvested and dried and then sent to the extraction plant.[3]

Starting School

School brought challenges for Kolini as he adapted to the new disciplines and surroundings. In first grade when a larger boy attacked him, he got into his first fight. Because Kolini was able to defend himself, he won the respect of his classmates. He liked school, both academics and sports, in which he excelled, and he especially liked gymnastics. A representative of a soap-manufacturing company was passing the school one day and saw the children performing. Kolini did extremely well and was presented with a bar of soap as a prize. He was very proud of his achievement and ran home excitedly to present his prize to his mother.

Soccer was also a favorite pastime, and Kolini and the other boys constructed balls by wrapping layers of banana leaves together and tying them tightly with string. They played with their homemade balls, barefoot, in the red dirt of the region.

Kolini had a maternal great-uncle named Semurema, who took an interest in his welfare at this time, visiting him at school during his first year. He was both a Roman Catholic and a highly respected judge in the area. He was very kind to his young nephew, and one day he arrived at the school, took his young nephew aside, and gently trimmed his fingernails with a razor blade. This humble act of love impressed Kolini, and because of his uncle's example, he developed a deep love for children, always wanting to make time for them.

On another occasion Kolini was absent from school for several days, and this uncle came looking for him. He wanted to encourage him, making sure that all was well and that he would go back to his lessons again. It was common in Africa at this time for a child's attendance to be sporadic since there were no laws making schooling compulsory, even at the primary level, and many parents who were illiterate saw little need to educate their children. Even today in Africa many children do not attend school, especially in the rural areas, because their parents have no money for uniforms, pens, or paper.

Semurema discovered Kolini was avoiding school because he was afraid of being punished for missing Mass, compulsory in Roman Catholic schools. His uncle visited the headmaster, explained the situation, and Kolini returned to his studies. His uncle then began taking Kolini to Mass with him and his two children, and again Kolini was impressed by his uncle's love and kindness.

Kolini had to walk a long way to school, which included the danger of crossing a river. Kolini's mother had taught her son to walk on the same path with the older boys. She thought this would help him arrive at school safely each day, providing they walked through the river and did not try to jump it. But one day during the rainy season, when the river was swollen and fast flowing, Kolini slipped while crossing. His friend managed to grab his hand and prevented him from being swept away and drowned in the fast-flowing current. Once again, God protected him. It seems that God had a purpose for this boy.

However, not every story has a happy ending. As Kolini progressed and did well in his studies, the friend who had earlier saved his life became jealous of his success and began tormenting and bullying him. In Rwandese schools a child does not automatically progress from grade to grade each year but must attain a certain standard before going on to the next class. An eager young child able to attend school consistently can move ahead of an older child who perhaps does not have these benefits. Therefore children of a wide range of ages can be found in each class.

One day this boy, whom Kolini had overtaken in school, picked up stones and threw them at him. Although Kolini was physically hurt, the stones bruised far more than his body. He felt bitterness toward this older boy, and it wasn't until much later, when they met in Congo, that Kolini was able to forgive him for his unkindness and jealousy and thank him again for saving his life.

True Friendship

Pygmies are called the *Batwa* people and are often despised. A group of them lived in the forest behind the family home. From time to time they would visit Kolini's mother and ask for food. Being a kind woman she shared what she could with them, and they in return spent time with her young son.

One of the young Pygmies had attended school, which was very unusual for Pygmies at that time. This young man took a great interest in Kolini and was able to help him learn his letters. With the help of this Pygmy friend, he was able to learn to read and write. His friend told Kolini folklore stories, which he can still remember more than fifty years later. The Pygmies also supplied Kolini with bows and arrows and taught him how to hunt birds.

At primary school he made a lasting friendship with a little girl whom he later learned was related to him through his maternal grandmother. The two stayed friends for many years. Kolini recalls making a list of his friends when he was in the third grade, and this girl was at the top of the list. He once commented that some friendships would always have an element of self-interest, while others, like the one with this girl, are just pure friendship.

They were neighbors and walked to school together. All the schoolchildren normally brought food with them to eat at lunchtime, gathering together in small groups to share their food. In time the other children gradually formed new groups, but the two of them always ate together.

Some of the other boys became jealous of the friendship between Kolini and this girl. They began to tease them and make accusations about the friendship, saying that Kolini and his young friend were sexually involved. One day when the two friends were walking home, one of the boys became particularly aggressive toward them, taunting them and making false accusations. They were able to escape from him by separating and taking a longer path home. The aggressive boy, fortunately, took another path.

The children were quiet and sad about the whole thing as they walked the long way home together. Kolini said, "I wish God could come and settle the matter and make it clear that it is not true." The young girl replied, "It would be very sad if we had a wrong relationship, a sexual relationship, and were caught. But it is just a false accusation, so why do you worry?" She had made a simple analysis of the situation with wisdom beyond her years.

Kolini had learned a great deal about himself also. He began to admit that he cared about his reputation and credibility and realized that if he ever asked a girl for sex and she refused, she might easily spread the word that he was a person with loose morals. Because he did not want to let himself down or disgrace his parents and family, he resolved to be careful in his conduct, both in public and in private.

The incident cemented their friendship even more, and they continued to eat their lunches together. After she finished at primary school and left for boarding school, the families still had some contact with each other, and even though the children were at different schools, they saw each other when they went to Mass. But because of school rules, they were forbidden any physical contact, not even a handshake. On her first holiday from boarding school, she visited Kolini at his home. He had a surprise gift for her, a bracelet; she was very happy to receive it. Both sets of parents were also pleased with the continuing friendship, even though because they were related, any thought of marriage was quite unacceptable in Rwandese society. In due course both families fled to Congo, and their lives then took very different pathways.

Kolini's First Book

During his primary school days in the early 1950s, his parents bought him his very first book. It was a New Testament written in Kinyarwanda, the language of the Rwandese people. They bought it for him, not for religious reasons, but because someone was selling it and they had ambitions for their son becoming well educated. There were, of course, very few books available in the vernacular, so it was a treasure for him and a gift he greatly appreciated. As he read it, Matthew 24, a very difficult passage for a child to understand concerning Jesus' teaching about the fall of Jerusalem and the end of the world, made a deep impression on him. It was the beginning of his interests in spiritual things, and for him, it was particularly significant that his first book was the Word of God.

In 1957 when Kolini was twelve years old, his mother gave birth to another boy, a momentous event for his family. They named the baby Roger Hodari. Hodari means "brave" in Swahili. His father may have been homesick for Congo at the time and therefore chose a Swahili name. They were very happy, and there was much rejoicing for the addition to the family after such a long time.

It was a great sadness for Kolini's mother that she was not able to have a larger family. In 1959 Kolini's mother became pregnant again, and everyone was eagerly looking forward to the birth of the baby. In the eighth month of her pregnancy, she went into premature labor and delivered a stillborn little girl. It was a time of great sorrow for them all. In most African cultures it is important for a couple to have many children, for in time, these children will have to take the responsibility of caring for their aging parents because there are no pension plans or social security provisions for the elderly.

In Catholic schools, confirmation was compulsory in the fourth primary school year, but first Kolini had to be baptized into the Roman Catholic Church. He became a Catholic because of the influence of his uncle and the teaching in the school. Later that same year Kolini went through the sacrament of confirmation, which meant he had to learn the catechism and be able to answer questions about it. But no one asked him about his personal beliefs or commitment to the faith he was embracing.

During the celebration after the confirmation, Kolini's godfather became drunk. He also gave Kolini alcohol—but on an empty stomach. What should have been a wonderful event was marred when Kolini had a severe reaction and became ill because of the alcohol. He soon recovered, though, without any lasting effects.

Once confirmed, Kolini joined the Catholic youth movement and became captain of a small unit of ten boys. They were very proud to wear their uniforms and caps. Leadership qualities emerged as he took responsibility for this group.

Senior School Days

When his six grades of primary school were completed, Kolini moved into the senior school at Nyundo, some thirty-five miles from his home. He attended this school for a year and then for the next two years moved to Gisenyi, the town by Lake Kivu where he had lived as a small boy with his grandparents. Senior schools, almost without exception, were boarding institutions, mainly Roman Catholic, and staffed by priests. Kolini does not remember his parents saying goodbye to him as he set out to live away from home for the first time, but he does remember his grandmother's farewell. In the traditional way she said, "Meet with women, my son," meaning, "Don't meet men who are warriors and may attack you." It was a traditional African way to say, "Go safely."

Throughout his school life Kolini always tried to keep himself clean, however difficult the circumstances, and his bed neatly made. These were standards he set for himself. On one occasion the headmaster was short of soap and sought out Kolini to ask him if he had any to spare. The priest was sure Kolini must have a stockpile, because he always kept himself so clean. He had none to give the priest; in fact, just the opposite was true. Kolini rarely had any because his parents had returned to live in Congo and there was civil war there; Kolini was unable to go home to get fresh supplies at the end of the semester. He and his friend once shared their last bar, trying to make it last until the end of the term. They divided it into two halves, which they used sparingly. Even after walking in the dust and mud, they still preferred to wash their feet in water rather than use up their soap.

By the time Kolini went to senior school, he had begun a spiritual journey, seeking to know God for himself. Although there were many activities in the Catholic boys' youth movement that were interesting and educational, he was disappointed by the shallowness and lack of spiritual content. He saw little spiritual maturity in the majority of the priests that marked them out as men of God.

As he grew older, he began to think about things and reason them out for himself. One time in a religious education class he questioned the priest, "According to your teaching, Satan became Satan because he refused to worship God, who made himself man, but Jesus made *himself* man with the intention of saving man, who had sinned." The priest became angry and retorted, "It's just you who thinks that!" Then the priest turned on his heels and stormed out of the class.

But the following week when all the boys took their religious education examination, he awarded Kolini a perfect score, even though to this day Kolini is quite sure that he hadn't answered every question correctly.

Church and Politics

The political scene, as in many other places, was always changing in this part of Africa, where one group was friend while the other enemy. The Tutsi people were being labeled as communists, so Kolini, like many other Tutsi, was being discriminated against.[4] Inevitably, as happened with many Tutsi and their sympathizers at this time, an anger and disillusionment with the Catholic Church grew in him. He was losing respect for the church because of the prejudices that the leaders held. He began looking at Christianity as the *muzungu* religion, a propaganda that was being used to colonize, control, and "civilize" the native peoples. This made him angry, and although he still attended Mass each week, he felt less and less real commitment to the Catholic cause.

Even though the school insisted all boys go to confession, Kolini became more and more reluctant to go. Confession had to be made to the missionary priest, a White Father[5], not to the more trusted priests who were their teachers and would have given them more protection. One time one of the Tutsi boys pretended to be a Hutu and falsely claimed that he had killed a Tutsi and burned Tutsi houses. The missionary priest believed him and said, "Don't worry; killing a communist is not a sin because they are enemies of God." This boy boasted to Kolini about the attitude of hatred against the Tutsi that the priest held, which took away any desire Kolini had to confess to him.

He continued to read the New Testament his parents had bought for him, which caused his spiritual hunger to grow even more. But he still had many questions that remained unanswered, even when he asked them in school or church. The questions never left his mind, for God was drawing this young man to himself.

During this early journey with God, Kolini began to see that his main struggle was that he never really felt forgiven, even after confession and absolution. He did the penances required, but often in anger as he felt they were unfair. To him, God was a policeman who was always catching people sinning so he could punish them. Kolini had no concept of a God of grace and love. He felt it was time to leave the church. He had come to see the church as an anti-independence movement, merely another type of politics that involved very little that was either biblical or truly spiritual.

CHAPTER 2

Displaced in Congo

R̰wanda has been populated for centuries by three main people groups: the Batutsi, Bahutu, and Batwa. (*Ba* denotes the plural; one person is a Tutsi. This grammatical construction applies to the Bahutu and Batwa people as well.) The Twa people, who are the Pygmies and the least populous of the three groups, were probably the first inhabitants of the region. They were hunter/gatherers, and it is thought that they have lived in this part of Central Africa since the early Iron Age. Today they are better known for their skill as potters, than as jungle people.

Although the exact dates are uncertain, probably around 700 bc, the Batwa were joined by the Hutu people—Bantu-speaking agriculturalists who were spreading over Central Africa seeking good land where they could settle and begin cultivation. The Hutu began to use their iron tools to clear the traditional hunting grounds for farming use. They were a much larger and stronger group of people than the Twa.

The third group—tall, more slender cattle raisers, who raised their children on milk—was called Tutsi. Oral tradition teaches they arrived from the north or northwest around AD 900–1300. Through the generations, although the Tutsi were less numerous than the Hutu, a social hierarchy developed in which the Tutsi were seen to be superior to the shorter, stockier Hutu. The Tutsi became stronger and taller, probably because of more protein in their diet. Both of these groups looked down on the Twa.

All three ethnic groups spoke the same language and enjoyed the same culture, and intermarriage was not uncommon, so the typical physical features were often modified through the generations. There was also an upward mobility, as a Hutu could become a Tutsi if he owned ten or more head of cattle.

This small kingdom ruled by a Tutsi king was hidden away in the mountains of Central Africa and remained untouched by outside influences—the Arab and Asian traders who traversed so much of Africa and even the slave traders from the West—until the late 1800s. Until then the kings and their representatives were able to keep the peace, and it was easily defended from enemies because of the many hills and mountains and by intrepid *intore* warriors. Rwanda remained a secret and a closed country for centuries. But the beginnings of racial conflict came with colonization, first by the Germans in 1885 and then by the Belgians in 1919.

Rwanda was originally colonized by Germany during the latter part of the nineteenth century. In 1885 at the Berlin

Conference, under the name of Ruanda-Urundi, the country was assigned officially to Germany as part of German East Africa, although no Europeans had settled there. In fact, the ruling *mwami,* the Rwandese name for the Tutsi king of Rwanda, had no idea that his country was officially owned by Germany. The actual dates are uncertain, because as yet there were no written records, but it is thought that Rwanda had been a monarchy possibly since AD 1000. The Batutsi were the ruling class, and a very effective feudal system was in operation. It was the belief of most of the population that the *mwami* held some sort of divine authority. A legend says that the very first *mwami* was not born in the same way as other human beings, but was born from an earthenware jar of milk.

Cows and milk have played a great part and have always been revered in Tutsi culture. There were pagan, animistic religious practices and also a belief in *Imana,* the creator God, alongside the supposed magical properties of the *mwami.*

When the Germans did begin to enter Rwanda and settle there, they found a well-organized country that was feudal in administration; everyone had a place in the society, accepted it, and lived together in reasonable harmony. The colonialists also discovered a very beautiful and fertile land with so many mountains, hills, valleys, and lakes that it was called "the Switzerland of Africa." It was around this time in the volcanic Virunga Mountain Range that the first mountain gorillas were discovered, which became a source of amazement and interest to the outside world.

The Germans brought their own religion with them. The Lutheran Church, the dominant church in Germany, had not shown any great interest in evangelizing the new territory, so the Roman Catholic White Fathers were invited by the Germans to begin mission work. In 1884 they built schools to start educational work and hospitals and clinics for medical work, as well as churches. Some Protestant missionaries eventually arrived at the beginning of the twentieth century from the Bethel Mission in Germany, but they almost all left the country when Germany was defeated in the First World War.

The German administration also began its own educational program in 1907, with a nondenominational school that incorporated a military academy. It was established to educate the sons of the chiefs, most of whom were Tutsi, and was built near the royal palace at Nyanza in the center of the country. The colonial powers perceived that the children of the elite would learn more easily and become the country's future leaders, especially within the army.

They also quickly saw the benefit of pitting the Hutu against the Tutsi, and because the Hutu wanted to enjoy equal status and privileges with the Tutsi, tensions were fed and escalated, fueled particularly by the politics of the Belgian colonial government. In the 1930s the colonial government introduced a system of crude measurement of physical height and features, and by this they classified the population into "ethnic" groups, issuing identity cards and insisting that the populace carry them at all times. When it suited the Belgium government to change its pro-Tutsi policy and favor the Hutu, it began to stir up hatred among the Hutu against the Tutsi.

In the 1950s the Hutu leaders began to thirst for power and equal rights, seeking to end the old feudal system that allowed the Tutsi to rule. This claim in many ways was just, since the Tutsi still had the best educational opportunities and so took the best jobs.

The Hutu leaders wanted political change, and they had the backing of the Roman Catholic Church as well as more favor with the colonial regime. Elections were held in 1960, and the Hutu-backed party, Parmehutu, gained control, but this result did not stop the ethnic violence that had been unleashed.

Life was becoming ever more difficult for the Tutsi people. In 1960 five thousand Tutsi homes were burned in Butare; 22,000 people were displaced and hundreds killed. Altogether around 135,000 people fled Rwanda as refugees and exiles.[1] Large numbers were displaced to Bugesera, a region now called the Eastern Province of Rwanda, renowned for its swamps and swollen rivers, poisonous snakes, a range of diseases, and the tsetse fly. Bites from these little insects caused sleeping sickness, a life-threatening and severely debilitating illness. For this reason the region had never been highly populated, so sending Tutsi people there was like sending them to die.

But prejudice against Tutsi was seen in other ways as well. Places in senior schools, higher education, and any kind of higher-paying jobs were very hard for Tutsi to get or keep. Anger, fear, and frustration were growing within the Tutsi community as the ruling Hutu people group, the majority, made the lives of Tutsi people ever more difficult. So at the time Kolini was undergoing his education, tensions were beginning to boil over.

Expelled from School

In 1960 Kolini's family had been forced, because of the political situation, to relocate to Congo. As displaced people, they left Rwanda and crossed the border at Gisenyi into Congo, then known as Zaire. The family registered in the border town of Goma and found a place to live away from the actual town itself, though Kolini remained in Goma with his uncle, hoping to enroll in a school there.

In 1962 when Kolini was in the third year of senior school, he was told not to return. This was devastating news to such an ambitious and academically oriented student. To be expelled without any diploma seemed the end of all his dreams. He had come to believe that the only hope of improving his life and that of his family was to be well educated and find a good job. He was frustrated and angry and found it difficult to sleep.

Having left Rwanda without any formal educational qualifications, he knew he needed to continue his studies in some way. There was a vocational training school in Goma, and Kolini enrolled to learn electronics, for he thought it was better to study something rather than nothing. He was able to attend for only one semester, but it was a significant time for his spiritual journey.

Spiritual Journey

One day as he was walking past the Roman Catholic cathedral in Goma, Kolini heard a voice in Swahili say, "*Wenda umabudu Mungu Mwana*," meaning, "Go and worship the Son of God." He knew he had to obey, but he thought to himself, "There is no good God here!"

During the week that followed, Kolini prayed for the very first time a prayer from his heart instead of just reciting a prayer that he had learned or by reading the missal. This was a big step forward—seeking to talk to God for himself. The following Sunday, he went to the Baptist church in Goma, instead of the Catholic church with which he had by now become so disillusioned.

During the Baptist church service, an offering was taken. Kolini had only ten Congolese francs in his pocket, all the money he had at that time. However, he felt he had to give it all when the basket passed his way. After the service while walking home, he met a friend who gave him a hundred-franc note. Kolini was amazed. He was going home ten times richer than before he went to church! He felt that this was an illustration to him that God is no man's debtor and is faithful to hear and answer prayer.

Life in Goma

Despite this miracle the days were very hard and the nights were even worse because he couldn't sleep. There was a curfew imposed each day at four o'clock in the afternoon, and there were early morning raids by police and soldiers. It was an insecure place in which to live. One morning Kolini was arrested while standing outside a latrine. Only the intervention of his uncle got him released.

Many more Rwandese people were fleeing across the border into the relative safety of Congo, though each new influx made it all the more difficult for those already living there to obtain jobs or find food and shelter. Kolini's maternal uncle lived and worked in Goma and was a great help to his nephew by providing him with accommodations. However, this man then lost his job and had to leave the city for a nearby village, which meant that Kolini also lost his home in Goma. This added to his decision to return to live with his family in the country and try to get a place in a school there.

It was a hard decision to make because it meant giving up attending the technical school, which had been a place of healing for Kolini's battered emotions. But as he struggled with these choices, moving in the direction of leaving Goma, he heard a voice say, "If you are going to die here, you cannot complete your education! Live upcountry." So he returned to his family, who were living in a village.

There he enrolled in a local Baptist secondary school and began to regularly attend the adjoining church, even though it meant a two-hour walk from his home. The Baptist church also managed a large hospital at Beni. Kolini planned to graduate from the school and then apply for a place at the hospital to train as a medical assistant.

Despite these ambitious plans for the future, he felt stressful and was still unable to sleep. His uncle had found work on a coffee plantation, and Kolini joined him in the mornings and then spent the afternoons reading his books, crouched behind the door of the small, round mud hut. During this time, he visited a friend, a cousin of his childhood primary school friend and also distant relative of his maternal grandmother. This was one of the few periods of relief from his emotional stress, as this young woman, exiled from her homeland too, was very lonely and struggling to relate to her peers in this new land.

When he visited her, they were able not only to talk in their mother tongue but also to freely express their anger and pain. She was having some problems with a boyfriend and needed a brother to talk with. They developed an intimacy between them that was easy to misinterpret, and others misconstrued the friendship, including the boyfriend. Things became tense with the boyfriend and likely would have led to a fight, but it was averted before it came to that.

The times of just sitting and talking together brought inner healing to them both. It was the one bright star in the dark sky of the months while he was in exile in Congo. Kolini did not find such friendship and happiness again until years later when he was working in a refugee camp in Uganda.

At the Baptist secondary school where Kolini had enrolled there was insufficient money to feed all the children, so pupils were permitted to find work outside the compound. Kolini had his job on the coffee plantation, the salary of which was three hundred francs a month. His entire first salary was spent buying the simplest edition of the Bible. This was the first time he had owned a complete Bible, and to have a Bible of his own was a real joy; he began to read it enthusiastically. Also, during this time others began to see qualities of trustworthiness and leadership in him, and he became the school treasurer.

National Unrest

As Kolini grew in his spiritual journey, he sometimes heard a voice speaking to him, and he began to realize this was the voice of the Lord. For instance, one day at church the congregation was singing a song based on Matthew 11:28: "Come to me, all you who are weary and burdened, and I will give you rest." He heard a voice encouraging him, "If you are worried about things, then talk to Jesus." This was a special message at a time when everything was in turmoil politically and he was living as a displaced person with few rights and even fewer prospects. To be invited to bring every worry and problem to the Lord in prayer began to shape him into a man of prayer.

On another occasion Kolini heard the voice of the Lord speaking to him one Sunday morning as he was walking to church and saw a snake. Getting a large stick, he struck it on the head and killed it. Having done this, he heard a voice saying, "If you want to be a good Protestant, why do you kill? You have to be loving and compassionate." He questioned God, "Isn't it all right to kill a snake that might kill you?" He wanted to understand God's will because if he were to be a Protestant Christian, it meant obeying God's Word.

He was soon to discover that the question was relevant in other ways, because of the developing situation. In September of that year, 1964, Congo was plunged into a bloody civil war, the Simba Rebellion. One of the key leaders was Murere, which is why the rebellion is sometimes referred to as the Murere Uprising. This revolt lasted for two years and was the climax of a very troubled history in this region.

The Democratic Republic of the Congo, as it is now called, is a huge Central African country covering 900,000 square miles. When the war started in 1964, the population numbered only around fifteen million, and it was proving to be an almost impossible country to govern because of its vast size.

As was stated before, many mistakes were made in the colonial era that contributed to the harvest of bloodshed that occurred in later years. As far back as 1885, when the country was known as the Congo Free State, King Leopold of Belgium annexed the entire country as his personal estate, which of course included all the mineral wealth of gold and diamonds. In 1908 the Belgian government began to administer the country as one of its colonies and built cities, plantations, schools, roads, railways, and hospitals, providing the infrastructure and bureaucracy needed to support these ventures. But along with this provision there continued to be both an unacceptable exploitation of the indigenous peoples and a plundering of the country's wealth.

By the dawn of the 1950s, even though there were still very few educated Congolese, the populace began to lobby the colonial government for independence. This developed into a rebellion led by Patrice Lulumba, aimed at throwing off the Belgian yoke and demanding that all *wazungu* leave the country.

The Belgian government responded very quickly, and on June 30, 1960, it granted independence to the country. But in many ways the country was not prepared for self-rule. Elections were duly held, and Patrice Lulumba was voted in as the new prime minister, but after just a few months in office he was deposed and killed. This led to disarray in the country, with hostility breaking out among differing political and tribal groups.

In Shaba district, where Kolini was later to serve as bishop, Moise Tshombe was the governor. He tried to break away from the central government and make the province independent. The United Nations intervened, quickly crushing the uprising and banishing Tshombe from the country. He fled to Congo Brazzaville, which had previously been French Congo.

After Patrice Lulumba's ousting and murder, three more prime ministers tried to bring peace and unity to the country, but their times in power were short lived. Unrest and riots were developing in different parts of the country; Kwilu, Lomani, and Kivu provinces were all affected.

A new dissident rebel group sprang up and made its headquarters in Brazzaville and in 1963 called itself the National Liberation Committee (NLC). This was a subversive movement focusing on undermining and deposing the fourth prime minister. Before he left office, he invited the banished Tshombe to return to Congo and form a "Government of Public Welfare."

Tshombe agreed to do this, and on July 10, 1964, he was sworn into office. This man desperately tried to bring reconciliation and peace to his beleaguered country. He attempted to restore the broken economy and to prepare the country for lawful elections. He even opened the gates to the prisons and liberated more than two thousand political prisoners. He also made numerous gestures of peace, reaching out to the rebels and trying to restore them to society, but without success. The rebels began to attack the towns of northeast Congo, bringing fear and much bloodshed. Again Tshombe sought to meet the rebels' demands and bring peace, but they did not want peace and rejected all his moves toward reconciliation. Full-scale rebellion broke out in late 1964.

Many of the rebel leaders had traveled to communist China for training, including Murere, who, on his return to Congo, organized the *jeunesse* youth movement that proved so powerful and evil in its execution of duty during the rebellion. The strategy was simple; the rebel leaders would send a group of *jeunesse* into a village, shouting that the *simbas* were coming, a warning that the "lions" would soon arrive. They came with their bows and arrows, their spears and their guns, terrorizing the population and brutally forcing the villagers to accept the rebel regime, while enlisting all the young men into their ranks.

Young men like Kolini and his friends were particularly vulnerable because they were already in exile in Congo and could not return to Rwanda. There were also many poor people who had been disenchanted with the government ever since independence and who were easily enlisted into the rebel cause. Of course, you become particularly compliant when a gun is being pointed at you.

The rebels especially targeted the administrative centers, where the authority of government rested, to cause the most disruption. They also had a campaign to eradicate all *muzungu* workers, especially North Americans and Belgians. At least forty-four missionaries were murdered during this uprising. The rebels also built roadblocks and thoughtlessly killed anyone who opposed them. Groups of forty to sixty men roamed the countryside, raping and pillaging by force of arms but also threatening witchcraft to instill fear and submission into their victims.

During 1964 the Rwandese living in Burundi had also created a band of freedom fighters, calling themselves *inyenzi* (cockroaches). They linked up with Murere and the Congolese rebels. They were intent on gaining ground all the way from Burundi to Bukavu in Congo. The intention was to reach Bukavu and capture the city, which in turn would enabled the *inyenzi* to cross the river that formed the border with Rwanda. They would then march on Cyangugu, achieving a foothold in Rwanda, so when the freedom fighters had conquered and proclaimed their independence in Rwanda, they would then invite Murere to form a Congolese government in exile with the support of the king of Rwanda.

This plan failed, even with military help from Cuba and China, because Bukavu did not fall. The *inyenzi* were driven back into the mountainous southern region of Congo, the Shaba (Katanga) district, and were then captured. Prime Minister Tshombe of the Government of Public Welfare then issued a decree that all Tutsi in Congo should be arrested and put into prison. This included the whole Tutsi population—parents, children, and the elderly.

One Sunday all of Kolini's family members were rounded up for passage to the prison camp. In a strange way the timing of the arrest was a blessing, for that Sunday Kolini was due to return to boarding school after his vacation. Had he been either at school or on the way, his chances of survival would have been much reduced. As it was, he was not separated from his family. His young brother, Roger, was not able to walk all the way to the camp, so Kolini often carried him on his back. They walked for two days to reach the nearest administrative center where they were to be interned. This place was already full of Tutsi, so they were driven to a prison near the Ugandan border.

There was no room to house or feed all these people in conventional prisons, so they were allowed to live as families in villages within a certain area—a prison camp without walls or perimeters but with restrictions. The housing was very poor, and people were left to survive as best they could with no real freedom of movement. The whole family was interned like this for a month, though Kolini's one thought was to return to school as soon as he could and continue work toward his diploma. This proved impossible, as an order was issued to arrest all Tutsi young men, forcing them into the ranks of the Simba rebels. With the Lord's help, yet again, he fled to Uganda, where he lived with the family of a school friend.

Many Tutsi students at the university at Goma had been captured and targeted for elimination. When the plan to kill them was uncovered, a group of Tutsi men tried to intervene, but one of Kolini's uncles was shot as he tried to climb the fence and open the gates for these young people to escape. Many people were killed as punishment for the escape attempt.

CHAPTER 3

Escape to Uganda

Kolini had always intended to return to school as soon as possible and obtain his diploma to help him earn a good living. In his thinking, no education meant no certificates and no job, and without these he could not achieve anything. On being released from the internment camp, he reminded himself of what the Lord had said to him when he had to leave Goma and his schooling. While thinking, "Without these things, I am as good as dead," he had heard the Lord say, "It is not the end of the world for you."

Now looking back he can see, indeed, that it was not the end of the world for him. Instead, God brought about unexpected solutions to give him a much more fulfilling life. But at the time Kolini had to learn to trust God for his future because he saw no future for himself. Instead, everything had been taken away from him, with no possibility of returning to school. Now with four other young men, he planned to escape to Uganda to find work.

The civil war in Congo was intensifying, so he could not safely remain in the country. Neither was there any way that he could return to his homeland of Rwanda. To do so would mean certain death for him as a Tutsi, so it became clear that only one other option was open to him: he would escape to Uganda as a refugee. Three evenings he prayed, and when he was sure he was doing the right thing, he visited his uncle and told him his plan. It was to be a secret, but he asked his uncle to let his parents know where he was going. He decided to go with the other young men, and they made their plans carefully.

Very early one Sunday morning the youths began walking through the bush to Uganda. There were numerous roadblocks along the way, and these had to be avoided at all costs. Had the young men been caught escaping, they would have been either forced into the rebel army or shot. Yet they were unsure of where these roadblocks had been set up. They knew they could not go to the border crossing by the main road as it would be heavily guarded and they had no papers or passports, all their documents having been taken from them in the internment camp.

One young man in the group of five was especially nervous. They realized that as a group they would raise more suspicion than if they traveled alone or in pairs. To begin with, they joined in a group of people who were going along the road to the market. Here they did not look out of place mingling with the crowd. On arriving at the market they waited, then joined people leaving the market. After a while they realized that most people had reached their homes and that they were on their own once again. They decided that two of them should travel ahead, then the nervous young man would walk alone, and then the last pair of boys would bring up the rear. They devised a series of whistles to indicate which way to turn. In this way they could travel without causing suspicion, and no one would get lost en route. The only problem was they didn't know the best way to go.

Kolini had a maternal uncle who lived about halfway to the border. The plan was that they would stop at his house and ask him to guide them to his grandmother's uncle, who lived very close to the Ugandan border. They reached the uncle's house, only to find no one at home. Without guidance they did not know which route to the border was roadblock free. So Kolini went ahead to see if he could find a route and saw a woman at her home. He decided to ask her for directions but without raising too much suspicion, for in times of civil war it is hard to know whom to trust. A neighbor can be an enemy.

He greeted her in the customary way, and then he told her that he was a son of the man whose house they were trying to reach and that he was a student in Goma and was coming home to visit his father. He went on to say that he usually traveled by a certain route, but he could not go that way with all the trouble, and could she redirect him.

She told Kolini where the roadblocks were and drew a map for him, showing the way to the house of his relative. Armed with the map Kolini went back to his friends, who had been waiting some distance away.

The young men followed her instructions, Kolini being in the advance party since he had the map. The system of whistling worked well, and they did not get lost or separated from each other during the long trek. The group quietly and carefully walked to the house of Kolini's uncle, who received the young men with great kindness and made a meal for them even though he was quite elderly. Then he gave them each three Ugandan shillings to help them on their way.

To give away fifteen shillings was a huge sacrifice, and the young men were grateful. They had nothing except the clothes they were wearing, and the trek through the bush had not helped the condition of their clothes, but at least they were safe. He then allowed his own son to guide the group for six hours along the cow trails that led into Uganda and safety.

Safety at Last

Once in Uganda they headed for the home of one of the young men. His mother was living very near the border, and they were able to sleep there. They could not remain with her, for under Ugandan law they needed to register as refugees at the police offices. The following day they were on the road again and then reported to the police at Kisoro.

They were kept at Kisoro for a month and then transferred to a refugee camp at Kabale. Like them, many other refugees were coming over the border into Uganda from both Rwanda and Congo, so the camps were crowded and had no facilities for either cooking or hygiene. Most people had fled, leaving all their possessions behind before coming to the dusty, dirty camp.

They were usually set up in healthy areas to begin with, but with many people crowded together in shacks without proper sanitation, sickness and death were common. And the very enemies they had hoped to leave behind infiltrated the camps and began intimidating the refugees.

What Kolini learned later was that if he had not obeyed God's voice and fled to Uganda when he did, he would have probably been rearrested and imprisoned for the rest of the Congolese war, as were most others who were released from internment at the same time as he was. Once again he witnessed God's gracious hand on him, keeping him safe and guiding his way, even though he knew so little about God at this time.

Travel was permitted inside the large perimeter of the camp, but to travel outside the camp to find work, one needed a permit. With all their documents having been taken, Kolini and the four other young men were therefore restricted to the camp and unable to work outside. The only clothes they owned were those they were wearing, so they could not take them off to wash them. Kolini had lost so much weight that his trousers no longer stayed up. He decided to walk by the tailor's shop and pick up the small pieces of discarded material and somehow weave them into a belt. This he did, although his trousers were still thin, worn, and very dirty.

But he also had other problems. He had no comb for his hair, so for almost three months it was matted. He hated not being clean, and the lack of hygiene meant his hair became infested with lice. All he could do was wash his hands and feet in a little water. Some of the girls in the camp became concerned about him and asked him, "Why don't you comb your hair?" He replied, "The day I can wash my clothes will be the day I comb my hair!" His high standards of cleanliness and hygiene made it difficult for him. He even thought of returning to Congo to live with an aunt who had a house near the border.

One day, the headmaster of the Anglican school in Kabale came to the camp and brought with him a bundle of shirts that he had been given for the refugees. Many people quickly ran up to him, hoping to be given a shirt, but Kolini stood back and just watched. The teacher noticed him and threw him a shirt. What a wonderful gift! He could now wash his filthy shirt and wear a clean one.

One of the four young men who had escaped with Kolini had a brother who was living in Uganda and working as a policeman. He came to the camp to visit one day and gave his brother a pair of trousers and a shirt. From that time on the five friends took turns wearing the extra pair of trousers while they washed their own.

The young men also took turns cooking for themselves. When it was Kolini's turn, he didn't even know how to make the fire. An old woman took pity on him and showed him how to do this but did not stay to teach him how to cook the *ugali* porridge made from maize. Instead, she sent some young girls to help him, shaking her head and muttering, "What kind of young man cannot cook! He must be spoiled!" Coming as he did from a very small family, Kolini had not learned these skills.

Life was extremely hard in the camp. The young men owned nothing and lived in constant fear. There were Hutu spies in the camps, and Kolini and his friends felt a continual threat of being abducted and killed. Although they were safer living in the camp than in either Rwanda or Congo, their safety was by no means guaranteed. Not all Ugandans were pleased with the influx of refugees. Some Ugandans had been living in the area designated for the camp and had been expelled from the area to make room for the camp. And they also had their own political troubles at that time—struggles that were to lead to the bloody regime of President Idi Amin. Rumors spread that all the refugees were being sent back to Rwanda.

During Kolini's time in the refugee camp at Kabale, the Lord again spoke to him, saying, "After these bad times there will come good times." Even though Kolini had not prayed since the three nights before he left Congo and had not attended church, God had not deserted him. This was a welcome word of encouragement when everything looked so bleak and despairing.

While Kolini was in Kabale, his parents had also felt increasingly unsafe in Congo as the war progressed. When his mother became very sick, they also decided to join the many others going to Uganda as political refugees. But this time Kolini's little brother, Roger, did not have his strong older brother to help him along the way.

The family was taken to a camp called Kinyara, in the Masindi district of Bunyoro, close to Lake Kioga. When Kolini heard about this, he was able to leave the Kabale camp and join his parents. His parents were so glad to see their son and welcomed him into their very overcrowded hut, helping him even more by giving him a shirt. He decided to find a job to help his family, but no work existed.

Finding His Vocation

In the Kinyara camp, Kolini was able to attend one of the local church congregations, and the leaders there encouraged him. At last he had found a spiritual home that would help him mature in the Lord. His parents were still unbelievers but did not discourage their son's spiritual journey. In this difficult time he began to learn to trust the Lord for all his needs. As he considered his life, Kolini had several options: to join the freedom fighters, seek further education, continue to look for work in the city, or volunteer as a schoolteacher in the camp.

There were many children in the refugee camp, and most were getting no education. They roamed around the camp, bored, undisciplined, and hungry. Theft became an occupation; they would steal supplies from the United Nations' relief stores and then sell them to the local Asian storekeepers, who then sold the stolen goods in their small *dukas*. Kolini was challenged about this situation by a lay evangelist named Silas Sibomana. This man had also sought refuge in the camp and would later become his father-in-law. Would Kolini be willing to teach these children who were losing any prospect of a better life because they had no education? This challenge was the beginning of what would become a lifelong vision to help children by providing educational opportunities for them.

Kolini realized that although he couldn't get a job and earn money, he could at least share his education with these children, teaching them what he knew. He also had a friend who wanted to start a school. There was already a Catholic school in the camp, but none for Protestants. The two friends agreed to teach the children free of charge because the parents had no money.

At first there was no building, but soon the local Anglican congregation leaders offered the use of some of their premises. The school started without any supplies or equipment, and there was opposition from some of the older people in the camp who wanted the government to provide a public school for the children. Others tried to physically prevent pupils from attending either the Catholic school or the Protestant school. But the children so wanted to go to school that they devised schemes to evade these adults. Kolini tried to make the classes fun with lots of games and singing, and he also taught them the small amount of English he knew.

The school started with about one hundred children meeting in an outside shelter, but soon the shelter had to be demolished. The church leaders then allowed the school to meet in the church building itself. The friend who had promised to help with the school got married and had to look for work to provide for his family.

So Kolini became the only schoolteacher, and as the school quickly grew, he divided the children into two classes and looked for another volunteer teacher. There was a young man in the camp, John Rucyahana, who had been at the same secondary school as Kolini at Gisenyi. He was willing to become the second teacher. A very special friendship grew between these two men and in later years between their wives, as they continued to work together in ministry in Uganda and Rwanda.

With no equipment and just one church building, it took ingenuity to teach just one class, let alone two, so they rearranged the classroom with half the children sitting on wooden benches facing one teacher and the other children facing the opposite way toward the other teacher. They were able to successfully teach without the classes distracting each other. Because neither teacher had a watch, Kolini watched the sun's movements to tell the children when school was over.

In Uganda, schooling was conducted in English, whereas in Congo and Rwanda teaching was in French. Kolini had learned some English while he was in school, and this was helpful. He learned languages quickly and was fluent in French, Kinyarwandan, and Swahili. While living in Uganda, he quickly applied himself to learning more English so he could teach it. John taught first grade, and Kolini taught second and third grade. Kolini had one small blackboard on the wall, which he divided in half with writing exercises for the second grade on one-half and for the third grade on the other.

When the school started, the parents were not very interested in what Kolini was trying to do, but he quickly built the reputation of the school on three principles: discipline, cleanliness, and hard work. Discipline was particularly needed because many of the children had learned to steal while living in the camp, but the strict rules brought positive results, and this in turn helped the parents to appreciate and trust what Kolini was doing with their children.

If children arrived at school with *jiggers* in their feet, the teachers dug them out, putting tobacco juice in the wounds. This was an effective, though unpleasant, remedy. Jiggers are small fleas very common in dry parts of Central Africa. They live in the sandy soil and are a particular problem during the dry season. The female burrows her way into cracks of the skin and deposits her eggs.

Bare feet are especially vulnerable, and few refugee children had any kind of footwear. The flea's presence is very unpleasant, and the irritation can keep the victim awake all night. At first it is almost invisible, but after a few days the eggs swell into a mound the size of a pea. When they reach this stage, it is easy to remove them, but the cavity quickly becomes septic. Tobacco juice works as an antiseptic. Without treatment the feet become so inflamed that walking becomes impossible.

Inspections were also held regularly to ensure the children were free as possible from head and body lice, as well as scabies. These infestations were also very common in the refugee camps because of poor hygiene and lack of washing facilities. The school grew in both reputation and numbers, and more staff members were recruited. Within a few years there were four hundred students, five teachers, and a young woman who helped the girls in matters of female personal hygiene.

The school was given a small piece of land on which they were able to grow maize and cotton, which they were able to sell. With the proceeds Kolini was able to buy school materials, such as books, pencils, blackboards, and chalk. For many years the staff had no salary but worked on Saturdays and during the school vacations to earn a little money. When the school became well established, a small fee was charged for admission to buy supplies, but the staff remained unpaid.

There was a time when Kolini asked for a leave of absence as he needed to find work for a couple of months in order to buy himself some clothes. He especially needed some trousers because his one and only pair had disintegrated into holes. He felt it was inappropriate for a headmaster to be wearing trousers full of holes. When his predicament became known, he was given a gift of sixty shillings by one of the relief agencies, and he bought himself some clothes and plastic shoes. This agency, later, began to provide a little money for salaries.

Kolini remained as the headmaster of the school for a couple of years, providing both leadership and pastoral care. He was also growing spiritually himself and wanted to share this with his pupils. Each day started and ended with prayer, and as he preached the gospel, many children accepted Christ as Savior and friend.[1]

A revival meeting was held in the local church in the refugee camp. Although Kolini was sharing the gospel with the children in the school and was growing personally with God, he had never openly made a personal confession of faith. On December 5, 1965, he stood in the revival meeting to make a public confession of his faith, accepting Christ's sacrifice on the cross for the forgiveness of his sins. This public confession was significant in Kolini's life, so he also took that date, December 5, as his birthday. Not even his mother knew the exact date of his birth, so each year he is reminded on this day not only of the years passing but also of his new birth, making him a son of the King of Kings.

Kolini went back to school and shared this experience with the children. The Holy Spirit took up his words and moved among them, and about two-thirds of the children gave their lives to Christ at that time. The parents began to notice the difference in their children and were even more supportive of the school; some even became spiritually hungry themselves. As the children grew stronger in faith, they formed groups and began to evangelize the camp.

Ministry in the Refugee Camp

Kolini was not only spreading the gospel in the school but also assisting the lay evangelist from Burundi to minister in the refugee camp. John, his friend from school days and colleague at school, was also part of the team, and they created home cell groups throughout the camp. There were about ten thousand refugees in the Kinyara camp, so it was no small task to evangelize them. They were needy people and hungry for any good news yet were also hurt and damaged by the pain of their past and present situations. The three men would organize speakers to preach, and sometimes the children from the school would also give testimonies and share their stories.

In time Kolini gave these young students more leadership training, and they dispersed to preach the gospel. Amazing times of fellowship developed as people believed the gospel and worshiped together in the tradition of the East Africa revival brethren.[2] The youth ministry made a great impact on the camp, as children were often more ready to receive the gospel than their elders. Many of the older generation were full of anger, particularly those who had been Catholics in Rwanda, because they felt betrayed by the church. Over time many of these people were restored to the Lord, though because the ministry was under the umbrella of the Anglican Church, large numbers were baptized and joined the Anglican Church of Uganda.

Kolini, John, and the lay pastor were also involved in pastoral care, seeking to live the love of Christ. Sometimes a child would come to school and tell the teachers about a relative who was sick or in trouble, so a teacher would visit the home and pray with those in need, giving what little money they had in order to relieve the situation. The love and care they exhibited drew people to both the Lord and the church.

Through the years, as Kolini was searching to know God in an intimate way, his parents were watching him, noticing the changes in his life. As his life began to change, Kolini no longer wanted to drink beer. Roger, his younger brother, also stopped drinking, though not because he followed Christ, but he was in the school and wanted to obey the rules. In the end his parents stopped brewing banana beer. Home-brewed beer was the cause of a lot of drunkenness among the refugees.

Kolini's mother had always loved children and was disappointed that she never was able to have more children. When Kolini became involved with the young people in the Kinyara refugee camp, she was pleased as her home filled with young people. She had always longed for this and took great delight in welcoming the young people and cooking for them. This helped her find healing for her own personal loss. When giving her testimony some years later, she spoke about her sadness at having so few children and how the Lord had given her so many to care for.

In the camp Kolini's mother kept chickens. She had about fifty and generously used them to feed the young people who came to her house. When the meal was over, she and her husband would join the meetings. After some hearty singing of choruses, members would give testimony to God's goodness in their lives, repenting of any known sin. Kolini's parents listened to the testimonies, and the day came when his mother repented of her sin and accepted Jesus as her Savior. Not long after, his father also decided to become a Christian.

While Roger was a student in primary school, he too made a commitment to follow Christ. He went on to senior school but found it hard to keep his commitment. Some time later he returned to Congo and was arrested as a political prisoner. He had been visiting some school friends who were in the Rwandan Patriotic Front, the army that eventually liberated Rwanda during the genocide in 1994. Though not part of this army, he was accused, arrested, and imprisoned. God mercifully spared his life, and he was not executed.

During this time he grew close to the Lord again and worked as a volunteer chaplain to the other prisoners. He read the Bible and prayed with many prisoners. One of the prison officers was a Christian and met and prayed with Roger each day. Eventually he was moved to another prison and was expected to walk a long distance to reach it, despite a bad leg wound. He commented, "I missed my big brother because he would have carried me on his back as he had done when I was small."

A Continuing Friendship

About this time, Kolini was able to renew his friendship with his friend from early school days. A long time had passed, and they had not seen each other until 1965 when a mutual friend visited her and she inquired about Kolini. By this time she was married to an imprisoned government official and was staying with his relatives. When she discovered that Kolini was in an internment camp near her, she was determined to find a way to visit him.

It would have been too dangerous for her to walk alone to the camp as rape was a real threat during the Murere Uprising, especially by the soldiers who roamed the roads and villages. However, nursing mothers were respected as life givers and so were safe from such attacks. She borrowed a baby from a friend for the day, and with the baby strapped on her back, she made the journey to visit him.

The two friends were delighted to see each other again, catching up on the details of their lives after so many years. The camp internees were allowed to travel around within a prescribed area, so Kolini could accompany her back, ensuring she safely reached her home. When they arrived, the family invited him to stay as their guest, so Kolini stayed with her family for a while until he was able to escape into Uganda.

Many years later, he saw her again when he returned to Congo in 1981. They reminisced about their primary school days, especially about their teacher, her uncle, who used the cane a great deal when disciplining them both. Kolini commented to her that this punishment had probably done them both a lot of good. Her reply was to reveal for the first time that this uncle had then had an illicit girlfriend and was probably trying to intimidate them into silence.

To Kolini, this girl always seemed to behave with maturity and integrity and had provided for him a good example of young womanhood. This friendship also helped him throughout his ministry not to automatically assume that a relationship between a boy and a girl would always be sexual in nature. He now knew that it could be a true and lasting friendship without the sex.

Reflecting on all his school years, Kolini said he had learned important life lessons concerning friendship. The friendship with this young woman helped him define his own life principles and to think through the qualities he would look for when he eventually chose a wife. He knew it was not just purity of body he should look for, but also for someone who possessed qualities of orderliness, cleanliness, and integrity, which were important to him as well.

CHAPTER 4

The Call to the Ministry

In 1966, while Kolini was living in the Kinyara refugee camp, the archbishop of Uganda, who was also the bishop of the area, the Most Right Reverend Eric Sabiti, visited the church there and preached a message of encouragement based on Isaiah 40:1, "Comfort, comfort my people." As a pastor, he was sensitive to the needs of the refugees and actively searched for Rwandese men and women who would be willing to minister to their own people as lay evangelists and priests. Kolini felt challenged by his teaching.

The school was functioning well, and it seemed time to move on. Kolini had an increasing desire to do more evangelism in the refugee camp, and to do this work effectively he felt he needed to have some focused Bible training. He talked with the archdeacon of the diocese, Swithin Nyarubona, and with the blessing of this man, he applied and was accepted to go to college for a year of study. John Rucyahana[1] took over as the headmaster of the school.

Kolini began his studies at the Bishop Abel Balyar College in Fort Portal, Uganda, with another friend from the refugee camp. The course of study involved training for evangelism. Along with the valuable teaching and training at the college, Kolini learned that the cause of Christ is greater that any denominational division, and he also learned that he needed to forgive the Belgians and the White Fathers whose politics had caused such harm within his beloved country.

During this time at college, he had a supernatural experience of God. One night in the dormitory he saw a brilliant light coming through the window and heard a voice speaking to him, saying, "Today the light will shine on the college." He did not share this revelation with his two roommates but waited to see what the new day would bring.

The day passed as normal, but then after the evening worship, one of the students started to publicly confess and repent of sin. Following this confession another four students also came under the power of the Holy Spirit and confessed their sin and their need of a Savior.

This is how one of Kolini's two roommates, Bishop Geoffrey Rwubwsiri, later recounted the story:

It was 1967 and we were at college in Fort Portal. I had been sent for training from the same diocese as Kolini, but I came from the western part, from Toro, and he came from the north. We were put into the same dormitory, and Kolini occupied the bed by the window. He not only shared the dormitory, but he also constantly shared the gospel with me in a very quiet, gentle way. We became friends, partly because we both spoke Kinyarwanda as our first language. Although I am a Ugandan, I come from Kisoro, an area that at one time belonged to Rwanda until after the First World War when it was given to Britain. Kinyarwanda, the language of Rwanda, is spoken there. I come from the ethnic Hutu grouping, and I am short!

Peter, the other fellow in our room, was a believer too. Me, I definitely was not born again! No way! I had gone to college just to get some more education in the hope that it might lead to a job in the church. It didn't worry me that I had no real faith; it was a means to an end.

Then Kolini started to talk to me and I enjoyed listening and debating with him. He had an organized mind, which I appreciated, and he also understood my socialist ideas because in the past he had embraced them. I hated the colonial powers and what they had done to our countries, and I hated their God. In my mind, GOD meant "Go overseas and divide" or "Go overseas and destroy!" I was angry with the church and felt it had come as the White man's gospel and a means of subduing the natives. However, I was not beyond using the church as a means to get further education!

Let me tell you about the time when Kolini saw the light. He slept by the window and had seen this incredible light and had an encounter with God that night. Then, as you know, students started repenting after prayers. It was ten o'clock at night, and we were back in the dormitory and ready for bed. I knelt down to pray; I did not want Kolini to preach at me anymore. I think my prayer said something like that! In fact, I had organized that if he were to preach at me again that night, then a group of us would beat it out of him that very night. Who was he? Just a young boy who had accepted the White man's God!

That night he did not say a word. I lay down and then heard a voice speaking to me words I recognized as being from the Bible. They were from Romans 10:3: "If you don't believe in God, you have created your own God!"

I thought it was Kolini speaking to me. The lights were out, and we were supposed to be asleep. I looked at him, and he was very quiet, so I covered my face again with my blanket and drifted off to sleep. Then I heard the voice again calling, "Geoffrey, Geoffrey, even if you don't believe in God, you have created your own God!"

I was instantly awake and thought that Kolini must have arranged with some of the other Christians on the campus to gather outside and call me! I covered my face again and tried to sleep, but the voice called again, saying the same words. A bit like Samuel of old, I then responded, "You know, God, I hate you, I don't want you in my life, but if you are the one talking to me, I will allow you into my life!"

I found that I was out of bed and on my knees, I don't know how, I just was. I was accepting Christ as my Savior. I felt a huge burden like a rock fall off my head, and joy began to flood me! I woke up Peter and Kolini; I had to tell them what had happened to me!

That is how Kolini came into my life and in a way I am his spiritual son. We spent the year together and became firm friends. Our paths separated in 1980 when Kolini went to Congo. I married Mary, a Rwandese girl, and subsequently I was ordained into the ministry of the Anglican Church and worked as a parish priest in Uganda.

It was to be many years before Kolini and I were to meet again, and that happened in 2001 when I was consecrated as a missionary bishop from Uganda to serve in Rwanda and was enthroned the Bishop of Cynagugu. [Cynagugu is the southwestern diocese that borders Congo by the side of Lake Kivu. It is a very beautiful area, and Bishop Geoffrey has been used in a mighty way to build the church in that area.]

One thing I will say about my friend Kolini: he hasn't changed since I first knew him. He has a heart to preach the gospel, a loving and caring heart. We kept in touch through the years by letter writing, but never dreamed we would one day be on the same team, brothers together in the House of Bishops [sic].

Not long after the genocide when we had all come to Rwanda, we were at a meeting organized by AEE (African Evangelical Enterprise). The meeting was about healing the ethnic divisions. Kolini was on the platform with Canon John of Mid-African Ministries. I pointed to the two men and testified to the fact that they had never argued with me, even though I was Hutu and they were Tutsi. All our children were friends and visited each other; they were my dear brothers!

When I said that, they stood one on each side of me. Can you imagine, little me between those two big fellows? We hugged each other and sang "Glory, Glory to the Lamb," the hymn of the Rwanda revival.

Kolini spoke out and said, "Indeed, we have never known or felt that he was a Hutu and we were Tutsi!"

That word of testimony so touched the heart of one clergyman present that he repented of his ethnic hatred. He had a gun hidden on his person, just in case he needed it, and he surrendered it there and then!

It was while he was studying at that college and learning about evangelism that Kolini had a call into the ordained ministry. A Ugandan tribe called the Batoro people was living in the Fort Portal area. Kolini noticed that they had a custom of placing their hands on the heads of children as an affectionate way of blessing them. As he thought about this custom, he remembered the Catholic priests he had known in the past who had also blessed people by laying hands on their heads. Kolini longed to bless people in this way and felt that God was telling him that it was through the office of a priest that it should be done. That was the way he interpreted what he saw the Batoro people doing and was sure in his heart that the Lord was calling him into the ordained ministry.

Six months later he returned to the refugee camp because his studies were finished. He sought out his friend and counselor, the archdeacon, and told him that he felt the Lord was calling him into the Anglican ministry. This godly man sensed the hand of God on Kolini's life and recommended him for theological training for ordination. There was a great need for indigenous priests to work in the Rwandan refugee camps. Ugandan priests sometimes found it difficult because of the cultural differences. Three men were interviewed, two lay pastors and Kolini, and he was chosen for the theological training. There were no available places at the Anglican theological training center at Bishop Tucker College at Mukono, Uganda, or at the Anglican College in Nairobi, Kenya, so he applied and was accepted to study at the Canon Warner Memorial College in Burundi. For two years he studied hard in preparation for his ordination in August 1969. At age twenty-four he returned to Uganda for his ordination. During the previous year he had married Freda.

CHAPTER 5

The Love Story

F reda was the firstborn in a family that grew to have eight children. When the ethnic conflict escalated in 1959, her father, Silas Sibomana, was arrested and put into prison—his crime was that he was born a Tutsi. On his eventual release in 1962, the family fled into exile in Burundi and stayed there for two years before he was asked to go to Uganda and evangelize in the refugee camp. The Rwenzori diocese in Uganda hosted four large refugee settlements, two in Bunyoro and two in Toro. They badly needed help to minister to these people and recruited from Rwandese in exile in Burundi. One priest and two lay readers[1] took up the challenge; one of them was Silas.

Then in 1965 when Kolini had settled as a refugee in the Kinyara camp, Freda, now twelve years old, came with her family from Burundi. She was soon enrolled in the refugee school, and Kolini was her teacher. Although she was still a young girl, when he first saw her, Kolini recognized the voice of the Lord speaking into his heart, "There is a girl to marry!" "But she is young!" he answered the Lord.

In his personal life Kolini was struggling a little, because at twenty-one years of age, he, like most young men, wanted to get married. He had been looking around in the camp, and although among the ten thousand refugees there were many beautiful and eligible girls, he couldn't find one to suit him. It wasn't that the available girls didn't like him; some had been "making eyes" at him, trying to make him notice them. He remembered his acquaintances in Congo but then thought nobody would want him as a husband while he was still a refugee with no paying job or prospects.

He had made a promise to himself that he would not take a wife until he had one hundred Congolese francs saved and knew he could support her as a husband should. He wanted to be a responsible husband. In fact, Freda's father asked him once in 1966, "Kolini, when are you going to look for a wife?" His reply was, "When I get some money!" He thought that this older man just didn't understand his problems.

Later that year Kolini found that his thinking was changing. His father had acted as the official negotiator for the marriage of a relative of theirs, and this had somehow unsettled him. The Lord reminded him of when he had first set eyes on Freda and what he had said to him.

Kolini prayed about it, saying to the Lord, "Yes, she is very beautiful, but I am not marrying beauty. I want to know your plan and marry the girl who you have chosen for me. If it is Freda, then that's fine; but if it is not her, then that will be fine too." So he surrendered the matter into God's hands.

One night soon after this prayer, Kolini was awakened by a dream. The dream had two facets: he saw clearly that his name had been written in God's Book of Life, and he saw himself with Freda in a new house.

In the morning the dream was still very vivid in his mind, and Kolini sought out his two close friends, Peter Rukimirana and Ignace Rulinda, to tell them. The three young men had covenanted together to pray for each other. Peter had a gift for interpreting dreams and confirmed what Kolini thought God was saying to him through his dream. After this meeting the prayer burden he had been carrying concerning marriage to Freda disappeared.

In Rwandese culture, courtship and marriage are conducted rather differently than in the West. Things must be done in a certain order. Kolini knew after the dream that it was time to start the process. He faced a dilemma because Freda was his student and also still very young; but if he did not declare his interest, another suitor might approach the family first. His friends prayed with him and helped him decide the best way to approach Freda's family. He wrote a letter to her father, asking if he might be considered as a future husband. One day Freda found this letter, but she didn't say anything to Kolini.

The answer Freda's father gave to him was, "You will have to wait because she is too young." Kolini replied, "Yes, I know she is too young, but waiting is no problem for me. I am willing to wait as long as necessary, but I wanted to ask before someone else did." Kolini asked his friend John Rucyahana to act as the mediator between the two families because he was the godson of Silas and knew the family well.

In 1967, Kolini went home for a vacation after his first semester at Fort Portal College and felt it was time he talked to Freda. He told her his thoughts about marriage and asked her what her feelings and thoughts were. Her instant response was, "I need to talk to my father about this." Kolini also told her that he had not yet spoken to his parents about his intentions either and needed to know how she felt about his proposal before he took the matter any further. "If that is the way the Lord is leading you, if it is God's will, I will ask my father for his consent," she replied.

Then Kolini moved to Burundi for the start of his ordination training. When he arrived, he found to his surprise that he was the only bachelor student. The college professors strongly advocated that he should get a wife as soon as possible. They felt that priests should be married men and that their wives should receive training in the college to equip them for their role supporting their husbands in the parishes. When his training permitted, he went back to Uganda for a month to arrange all the introductions and wedding ceremonies.

Freda was just completing the last year of primary school. John was her teacher and headmaster as well as the negotiator between the families. In August 1968 Kolini and Freda married at the church in Kinyara. Freda was fifteen years old. The couple then moved to Burundi in time for Kolini to study for his second year in the theological college.

CHAPTER 6

Parish Ministry in Uganda

After Kolini had finished his theological studies in Burundi, he returned to Bunyoro and was ordained as a deacon in August 1969. The bishop felt it would be better for him to serve in another parish, which included a refugee camp, called Kyangali. Their home was not actually in the camp, so that they could be seen not as refugees, but as ministers to the whole parish, which included Ugandans. The parish was a large one to care for and presented him with many challenges. It was not in the Kinyara camp but near the other refugee camp at Kyangwali. The Kinyara area was a very dry and unhealthy area where mosquitoes and malaria thrived as well as a strange, untreatable disease called *burure*, which attacked leg muscles. There were also a large number of Kikuyu tribesmen from Kenya who had migrated to this area to grow maize and cotton.

About ten thousand Rwandese refugees were contained in the Kwangwali camp. When the refugee camp was opened in the area, there was a political move to spur the development of roads, schools, and clinics. The reasons for sending the young couple there were partly social and partly political. There was hope that if they helped to develop the area, the government would keep its promise to build roads and schools and help the area economically. There were other problems as well. Kolini and Freda were to live in a village called Bugoma. The area was known for witchcraft and cannibalism. It had been an almost abandoned area, isolated by Lake Albert and the Bugoma forest and game park around its perimeter.

Within his ministry Kolini had three groups of people to care for, each one having different needs and sometimes different languages. First, there were the refugees of Rwandan origin from both Rwanda and Congo, like himself. They spoke Kinyarwanda and Swahili. These refugees were also French speaking. Then there were the Ugandan nationals speaking Runyoro and Luganda. Finally, there were the economic refugees who had come from Congo, not seeking political refuge but to grow cash crops like cotton and tobacco in order to earn money and make a better life for themselves. These people were also Swahili speaking and felt very much at home with Kolini because he could speak their language.

The parish consisted of seventeen churches within a radius of fifty miles of the headquarters. Within this parish was an area of twenty kilometers of the Bugoma game reserve, north of Hoima, in the Bugoma forest, which borders Lake Albert.

Visiting the churches and parishioners meant trips on a bicycle through the forest. There was always the possibility of encountering buffalos and elephants, but the most problematic animals were the baboons that would just sit on the road and refuse to move, particularly if they had young with them. It was then a case of waiting, staying still, and praying that they would move. Early in the morning on one such journey, Kolini saw fresh lion paw prints on the road. He took off on his bicycle, pedaling for all he was worth and praying that he would not encounter the lion.

Many refugees were angry about their situation, including those in his congregation, and they took their frustrations out on each other. Kolini was very concerned. Although they claimed to be believers, they showed little real evidence of change in their lives and were constantly fighting and arguing with one another. He realized that he had to depend on the Lord continually for help and wisdom in order to intervene appropriately. One time a group of angry men tried to intimidate him by surrounding and questioning him. He told them that he would listen to what the Lord was saying to him, and then he would obey the Lord and not merely succumb to their demands. Kolini knew he was being tested to stand true to the Word of God and his principles.

He was still a young, inexperienced minister, and it was difficult to face such strong opposition from angry men. In time these men accepted what Kolini was saying and grew to respect him, understanding that he was a man of few words; but those words were thought out and measured, and Kolini always took time for prayer and meditation before giving any words of judgment. Gradually, Kolini learned to deal with these angry people and also to help the three groups relate to each other. It was a lesson in bringing peace and reconciliation, a lesson that would prove invaluable in years to come.

There was another huge challenge in his parish. The overseeing priest, Rev. Obaya, to whom Kolini was responsible, lived forty-five miles away in the Kinyara camp. He was not readily available to give counsel and advice to this young deacon. He came to visit and bring Communion only every three to six months. The positive result was that being on his own much of the time drove Kolini to his knees in dependence on the Lord rather than dependence on a priest, and the priest was very supportive and helpful when he did come to visit the parish. As a deacon Kolini was able to execute all the offices of the church except the celebration of Communion. He worked for a year under Obaya, and then on January 3, 1971, Kolini was ordained as a priest.

Kolini was like a missionary, having to live in a foreign land and learn a different culture. Although Uganda has borders with Rwanda and Congo, the cultures are very different, and it was not always easy to adapt or understand the ways of his Ugandan parishioners. Many of them showed sincere love and support for their minister, and they did not persecute or treat him in the way some Rwandan refugees were treated at that time.

Looking back on these years in the parish in Bugoma, Kolini realized that he learned by the grace of God to adapt, be patient, and become a friend to his people. This helped him absorb their anger, and he was able to encourage them to grow in the Lord.

Challenges of the "Reawakened" Movement

The ministry of the Church of Uganda was affected by a "reawakening" movement. A decade or so earlier the church had been deeply influenced by the East African Revival, "the Awakening," or the *balokole* movement. After a while, the momentum subsided, and a new movement then spread through the church. The new movement, while still emphasizing a close personal walk with God, had become very legalistic in its outworking. The archdeacon of the area, Swithin Nyarubana, a close friend and godly man, was involved in the new awakening. During 1970–1972 Kolini faced many challenges from this movement.

These brethren met every morning at five o'clock sharp for prayer and expected Freda and Kolini to join them. The group was very judgmental, often accusing nonattenders of backsliding, and was critical of those who were even a few minutes late. It was a huge burden for Freda because she was pregnant. Kolini tried to attend this meeting, serve the daily offices[1] of the church morning and evening, and also have his own quiet time with the Lord. His striving to do all of this was bringing him no joy or blessing. He was also physically tired from riding many miles each day on a bicycle to visit his parish.

One day another minister, realizing Kolini's struggles, challenged him. "Brother, tell me, which time doesn't belong to the Lord?" It was a release for Kolini as he realized that he did not have to meet the deadline of being up to pray each day at five in the morning, but that he could pray to the Lord anywhere and at any time.

These reawakened brethren also thought that no one should take out a loan. To do so, in their minds, was perceived as being greedy for money. It became a rule they imposed on others. Kolini had to think through this issue and realize that sometimes a loan was out of necessity, not greed. To ask for a loan when he needed a little money to get Freda to the hospital was not a sin.

The movement had so many rules about what could or could not be worn and could or could not be done that it brought a great deal of bondage to the believers. Having worked through these issues on a personal level, Kolini felt that he must stand against this sort of legalism that was stifling both the movement and also the Church of Uganda. For this reason he did not join the movement or encourage his parishioners to do so.

For example, one day the archdeacon challenged Kolini about his dog. Living in the bush as he did, the chickens laid the eggs that fed his children, and the dog guarded the chickens. This dog was a great asset to the family and a companion to their little boy. However, in the reawakened movement, it was thought that believers would trust in the dog to guard them, rather than in the Lord, so they had a rule against keeping a dog. Kolini asked the archdeacon if he really expected God to chase the thieves who might come and steal the chickens. He then asked the archdeacon if he had windows and doors on his own house. Were they not a form of protection? Was he putting his trust in the door when he locked it at night, rather than in God, to protect him?

Things escalated to such a degree that believers were refusing to talk to each other because of petty differences, and the church began experiencing division. There were divisions between Rwandese and Congolese, divisions between those from the north and those from the south, and divisions between different sects of the revival movement. Often Kolini suffered the brunt of their anger. They felt he was too young, and some despised him as a "northerner." The northerners were thought to be more backward than the southerners. Others criticized him because they thought he lacked spirituality, others because he did not support the revival group to which his father-in-law belonged and therefore he was not a good son.

Kolini did not want to be part of such things and stood firm to what he knew was the truth, even though it meant standing against some of his respected friends and colleagues. It was difficult, but as a pastor he could not allow some of these friends who were following the reawakening to preach any longer in the churches for which he was responsible. Some treated him as a backslider because he would not agree to all their rules and regulations. It was hard to be misunderstood, but Kolini knew he had to make a stand for what he knew was right.

It took three years to bring these factions together within the church, but the experience of passing through these difficult times made him stronger in his faith. He worked hard to disciple his people, bringing the Word of God to them faithfully and helping them to grow in their faith in and in the knowledge of Jesus. His parish was also his schoolroom in which the Lord was preparing him for future leadership where he would again take a stand for truth.

Freda's Story

Life was not easy for Freda in the early days of their marriage and ministry. Not only was she very young, but her background had been different in numerous ways. Freda had been born in 1953 in Gikongoro, a region south of Kigali, capital of Rwanda. Her parents were committed Christians and brought up their daughter and the seven other children to know and love the Lord. In 1959, when ethnic violence broke out in Rwanda, resulting in persecution of the Tutsi minority, her father was arrested and imprisoned, and Freda and the younger children stayed with their mother in Kigali. It was several months before he was released, and the family then decided to flee as refugees to Burundi. Freda was nine years old when this happened, and she still carries memories to this day of the horrifying scenes she witnessed on that journey. In God's goodness the family made it safely across the border without being attacked. They settled and lived there for three years, while Freda's father worked as a lay evangelist and boldly preached the gospel.

While in Burundi he was challenged about the spiritual plight of the thousands of Rwandan refugees living in camps in Uganda. When he was asked if he would be willing to evangelize there, he felt it was the Lord speaking to him. Even though these camps were notorious for poverty and disease, he was convinced he should relocate his family there. Friends questioned him about the wisdom of such a move, criticizing him for his plans to take his beautiful children there. His friends considered it to be a place of almost certain death for them. His reply was that he was going to do the Lord's work and that his children had already been given to the Lord. If the Lord chose to take them to himself or to spare them, then it would be all right because they knew they were in God's will.

When the family arrived at the Kinyara camp in Bunyoro, the conditions were very dire. Freda recalls her horror at seeing the rows of tiny mud and wattle huts with absolutely no sanitation. Food was scarce and of very poor quality. From time to time there were food rations brought in by the United Nations Council for Refugees, but it was never enough. Also, the Rwandese did not know how to cook the millet porridge, *posho*, which was the Ugandan staple food. Freda's family was accustomed to an abundance of food grown on the fertile hills of their homeland. Malnutrition was also a problem, especially among the elderly and the very young. Freda hated the hot, dry, desertlike conditions where mosquitoes seemed to thrive and malaria was rife.

At twelve years old she enrolled in the refugee school. One of her many challenges at this school was having to learn in English because her previous education had been conducted in French. As she told me her story, she laughed shyly and said her thoughts had been on her education, not on marrying anyone, especially her headmaster.

Once married, Freda faced the challenge of leaving home far behind her and traveling with her new husband to Burundi. The young couple was glad that no pregnancy occurred during the first year of their marriage, leaving Freda free to study and earn her diploma.

After Kolini's graduation and ordination, they moved into their new home, which was not in the refugee camp but out in the bush, quite a long way off the main road. This location was more central for reaching the seventeen churches for which Kolini was responsible, though it was quite a distance from both sets of parents.

As Kolini traveled around, getting to know his parishioners, Freda applied herself to the tasks of homemaking. Babies soon began to arrive in quick succession, since there was no family planning to help the young couple space the births. While they were in that parish, three children were born to them and then another three while they served in another parish before moving to Congo. Their last three of nine children were born in Congo. For the birth of their first baby, Christopher, Freda was able to get back to her parents in the Kinyara camp and have her family around to help, but it was a very different story for some of the subsequent births.

Freda had to battle with the isolation of living away from her extended family and also far from medical facilities. When their second child, Jeannette, became sick, it was two days before they were able to get a car and take her to the hospital. She was only two years old when she developed an acute abdominal problem with her bowel twisted. Kolini and Freda managed to get her to the main governmental hospital in the capital, Kampala, where she underwent surgery. The operation appeared to be successful at first, and she was discharged back into the care of her parents. It was soon very apparent that all was not well, so they rushed her back to the hospital. The surgeon decided that another operation was needed, but she died very soon after the operation. Together they mourned the loss of their precious child, Jeannette.

In Freda's third pregnancy, when the labor began, she had insufficient time and no way to travel to the clinic, and Kolini was unable to find a midwife to come and help. Freda delivered her child herself, a son they named John.

One night at the end of her fourth pregnancy, Freda realized that the baby was coming quickly. Kolini was very worried and asked, "What can I do? I cannot get you to the clinic, and I cannot leave you alone here!"

They considered the situation. The other two children were asleep, and there was no one near who could look after them. Freda decided she would stay at home, even though she was concerned about the labor and felt the birth would be a difficult one. She committed herself to the Lord and wondered if she would die in this childbirth. The couple prayed together and then tried to stay as calm as possible. When they welcomed the new little life into the world, Freda asked Kolini to cut the cord. He looked in horror and exclaimed, "I can't!" So she took the scissors and severed the cord herself. The next morning Kolini made the trip to the camp at Kinyara to tell their families about the new arrival, and some of them were able to come for a short visit to help Freda.

The nature of the parish work required that Kolini go on long journeys to visit his scattered flock. He was often away for a week or more, traveling miles on his bicycle. He had to make one such trip very soon after the birth of their fourth child, Harry (Heri, in Swahili, which means "blessed"). This left Freda to cope as best she could.

She missed having the family around her. Kolini recalls that Christopher was very slow to learn to speak because he was living in a nuclear family, rather than the usual extended family where grandparents and other relatives would have spent time developing his language skills. The only way to get to their parents in the Kinyara camp was either by an hour's bicycle ride or by walking, and neither option was possible for her with the small children. However, the families were very supportive of the work that the young couple were doing, and that was a great encouragement to them.

It was quite hard for Freda to make friends with her Ugandan neighbors, for although the women were friendly at church, the culture did not encourage visiting in the homes of those who were not relatives. Freda did make friends with the wife of the catechist, and they began to look after each other's children. In this way, the women could have some free time to go shopping or visit relatives. It was a sad day when this family moved away from the area, and Freda again felt isolated.

In 1971 Kolini made a trip back to Congo to visit his grandmother. It is interesting and also reflects the times that he was living in that his travel permit as a refugee allowed him to travel anywhere in the world apart from Rwanda and South Africa.

So he had no problems at the border when returning to Congo. While he was there, he met with an old friend who told him about the rapid growth within the Anglican Church there. He asked Kolini, "Why don't you come back?" It was a challenge that reached his heart and took root.

After Kolini's visit to his grandmother in Congo, an opportunity arose for him to go to Bishop Tucker College, the Anglican theological college in Mukono, Uganda, for a three-year period of study. Freda was able to accompany him and also take some classes. The college had a rule that students could bring only two children with them. Freda and Kolini then had three, but the rule was waived, enabling them to bring the whole family.

This was a defining time for Kolini, not just because of the further studies but also because he became acquainted and worked with Archbishop Janani Luwum, the primate of Uganda. He was a man of great spiritual stature who was fearless in his preaching, whether or not it offended the Muslim president, Idi Amin, who was becoming increasingly violent toward the Christian population. Kolini was with the archbishop on one occasion when he preached publicly, with loud speakers blazing out his message. He preached about the empty tomb of Jesus and the resurrection, comparing it to the gilded tombs of prophets whose bones still lay within them. With this, he sealed his doom. It was tantamount to suicide.

Luwum had been promoted from bishop of northern Uganda to archbishop of Uganda during the middle of Amin's cruel rule. While he was working in the north of the country, he had witnessed the disappearance of many friends and fellow

Christians. Some of his extended family were also killed during these years. He then became the archbishop and in his new position was fearless in defending his flock who were terrorized by Amin's army. Anyone who dared to criticize the regime incurred Amin's wrath because he was committed to eliminating any real or imagined threat to his power and rule. Luwum's outspoken criticism of Amin made him a threat. He personally confronted President Amin on more than one occasion, protesting the brutality of his soldiers. He demanded that the government live up to its mandate to protect the lives and property of the population.

In January 1977, Archbishop Luwum and Bishop Yona Okoth were accused of collaborating with three other people to overthrow the president and his government. On February 16, Amin called all the religious leaders to a meeting at the International Conference Center in Kampala. All the bishops from both the Catholic Church and the Church of Uganda were there, as were the leaders of the Islamic faith. Diplomats, cabinet members, and some senior military officials were all summoned to attend. Amin boasted arrogantly about a display of guns that was on view, and at the end of the meeting Luwum and two cabinet ministers were arrested.

Later that day Luwum was brutally tortured to death by some of Amin's henchmen who attempted to make the death appear to be a traffic accident. However, nobody was fooled. When details of his mutilation were testified to by eyewitnesses, the nation was shocked. President Amin's comment to Godfrey Lule, his then attorney general and minister of justice, concerning

Luwum's death was, "God has punished him." This evil dictator could not tolerate hearing the truth or having anyone stand up against him.

The day before Luwum's death, his wife, Mary, had begged him to leave the country, but he had refused to run away because he was not guilty of any crime. The next day, when summoned to the meeting at the International Conference Center, again Mary pleaded with him not to attend, warning him that if he insisted on going he would probably not return alive. His comment to her was, "If I die, my blood will save Uganda."

Indeed, just an hour or so before his death, Luwum and all the bishops at the meeting listened as Amin brought charges against him. He turned to Bishop Festo Kivengere, who was next to him, and said, "They are going to kill me. I am not afraid." It was his courage, dedication, and love for both his Lord and his people that inspired so many. From this brave brother in Christ, Kolini learned a great lesson about being fearless in all circumstances and of the need to speak against evil in public life. This was something which he would be called on to do in future years.

While Kolini was at Mukono, it was decided that he would benefit from some experience as an urban parish priest. There was a great shortage of ordained men in Kampala, so he was given the charge of a church in the capital, where he ministered for a year. Each Sunday the college paid for travel from Mukono to Kampala, a distance of about ten miles. The congregation was multicultural—Kenyans, Rwandese, Congolese, and Ugandans—so the services were conducted in both Swahili and

Luganda, often with singing in Kinyarwanda as well. With his background, Kolini was able to speak all three languages fluently, which was a great advantage.

While at Mukono, Kolini became increasingly sure that the Lord was calling him to return to and work in Congo, but the more he shared his vision with Freda, the more fearful she became. Congo was a foreign land to her. She had never lived there or even visited. She did not speak the language and felt very apprehensive. However, she knew that following the years of study, they needed to continue serving for another three years in the diocese; so she put the thoughts of moving to Congo from her mind.

But when this period of further study ended, the bishop appointed Kolini to a new parish, called Bulindi. The churches in the parish were places where people in the reawakened movement had caused a lot of problems. Many parishioners had left the church, and part of Kolini's task was to win them back. The believers, especially those who belonged to the reawakened movement, were very worried about Kolini being sent to them. They thought the bishop had sent him as a spy. It took a year for Kolini to make friends with these believers. He visited them in their homes, went shopping for them, and invited them to preach in his churches.

They gradually began to return to the church and bring their children and grandchildren for baptism. After three years it was time for Kolini to leave Uganda and relocate his work to Congo. These people begged him to stay and remain as their pastor because they had grown to love him so much. He explained that the Lord had called him back to his homeland to preach the gospel, and he must obey the call. For Kolini this season of learning taught him not to compromise, but to win people by love and by keeping himself close to the Lord.

Twenty years after leaving that parish, Kolini went back to the area and met again the archdeacon who had opposed him; they embraced and met as brothers in the Lord. The archdeacon then understood the stand that Kolini had taken. To have reconciliation and restoration as brothers brought both men great joy. This servant of God is now with the Lord, but in 1998 when Kolini was back in Rwanda, he made a trip over the border to visit him for two weeks. He was a man who loved the Lord dearly. He used to sing the reawakened songs, especially "It Is Accomplished" in the Ruankole language, which Kolini still remembers and sometimes sings himself, bringing back memories of this archdeacon.

But the days in Uganda were coming to an end, as God's call to return to Congo was becoming more insistent. The parents of both Freda and Kolini were still living in the refugee camp, as was Kolini's brother, Roger.

CHAPTER 7

Living Under
the Rule of Idi Amin

During the late 1960s, the people of Uganda had been oppressed under the presidency of Milton Obote. The dissatisfaction with him was so great that when a military coup took place in January 1971, the colonel in chief of the army, Idi Amin, was welcomed as a hero. He had ousted an unpopular leader and then released many of his political prisoners. It looked, therefore, as if Uganda was going to enjoy some years of peace and prosperity. This proved not to be the case. Even in the early months of the new regime, there were rumors of terrible events taking place within the army barracks and the civilian prisons. It was a foreboding of massacres that would begin in July of the same year.

Amin was the victim of his own unstable and, possibly, psychotic personality. He could be jovial and generous one moment, then utterly ruthless and violently unpredictable the next. He was nearly illiterate and politically naive, and within a few years he brought a once-prosperous country to its knees. His inability to write meant that he gave all his orders to assassinate verbally, and so there were no written documents to incriminate him later. Such orders would also be veiled. He would say, "Give him the VIP treatment," which meant, "Kill him after the torture."

Trade suffered as he wasted money on unbudgeted projects, with no responsible thought that one day his country would have to pay the bills. He was incapable of differentiating between personal and governmental expenditure and built his own personal empire using public money.

In August 1972, the Asian population, most of whom held British and Ugandan citizenship, was expelled in large numbers from the country. They had ninety days to leave and were forbidden to take any of their assets with them. They were allowed only one hundred US dollars in cash. For several generations the Asian population had run most of the businesses in Uganda, both large and small. Once they had left, Amin gave their shops and factories to friends, both army personnel and relatives whom he wished to favor. Many of these people were illiterate and totally unable to conduct business.

There is a story of a man who took over a clothes shop and, having no idea of prices, decided that the number he saw inside the collar of the shirts in his stock must mean the price of the garment; so he charged by size. Another story is told about a shopkeeper who would ask his customers what they had previously paid for an item and then charge them whatever price they said. His stock was soon sold off at bargain prices. Within months the country was in chaos, with no merchandise on the shelves, factories left to rust, and plantations overgrown. Pharmacies were emptied of drugs, sold indiscriminately to anyone who asked. All basic commodities such as sugar, salt, bread, and household goods were increasingly hard to obtain.

From 1973 onward there was a "brain drain," as educated Ugandans fled the country in the wake of the expelled Asians and Westerners. This meant there was no rising generation to take their places, and the schools, colleges, and universities did not even have pens and paper for their students. Life was grinding to a standstill.

Meanwhile the massacres continued, and Amin brought more and more Nubian Muslim Sudanese into ruling positions. Christians were marginalized and targeted for the death squads if they were outspoken against his regime, just as Archbishop Luwum had been.

Amin's troops killed hundreds of people and shipped their bodies in trucks to three main sites on the Nile: the Owen Falls at Jinja, the Karuma Falls in Murchison Park, and the Bujagali Falls. Here they were dumped into the river with the hope that the crocodiles would eat them. There were far too many for that, and bloated bodies remained in the water and on the banks for many months. It was a horrific time for the country.

Everyday living was obviously very difficult for Kolini at this time as he conducted his Ugandan ministry and Uganda's economy was spiraling out of control. The church gave Kolini a very small salary and no additional food allowance. Kolini bought a small piece of land from one of the schoolteachers and would cultivate it at five in the morning, in order to do his parish work on his bicycle all day.

On one occasion when the family had no food, they prayed and waited on the Lord to provide, which he did later that day. A farmer brought them food because as a member of the parish he wanted to provide for his priest. The custom and culture in Uganda is to show hospitality. This act of kindness both encouraged and amazed Kolini and Freda as they trusted the Lord for his provision.

When Kolini and his family were appointed to the new parish, they moved to a house on the main road between Hoima and Masindi. Although in some ways it was an advantage to live near the main road, it also proved to be a problem because it was a route that Amin's soldiers constantly patrolled. These soldiers had no respect for any civilian, being both trigger-happy and intimidating. As Amin increased his supporters by adding Muslim Sudanese soldiers into his army ranks, the anti-Christian propaganda increased, putting all believers at risk. Restrictions on movements and curfews from four o'clock in the afternoon were imposed on the civilian population, along with a complete blackout after nightfall. Not even the hospital was allowed to have lights. This made things increasingly more difficult for Kolini, but he still insisted on visiting his outlying churches and encouraging the brethren. Most of the village people walked through the bush tracks when they needed to leave their homes, but that wasn't a real alternative for Kolini, who had frequent and long journeys to make, so he rode his bicycle along the main road. Freda vividly remembers one day hearing an army truck coming along the road just after her husband had set off on a short trip. The truck pulled up, and the soldiers confronted Kolini.

"Where are you going?" they demanded. "Just half a mile down the road, and then I will be back," he replied. He started to ride away, and Freda heard a volley of rifle shots. She was sure he must have been killed or at least badly injured. But somehow, every bullet missed. Kolini continued his journey and arrived safely at the place he had arranged a meeting. He was talking with someone by a small shop, still on the Masindi road, when a second truck of soldiers appeared and began to fire at him again.

"Wow! They are serious about this!" he exclaimed and decided that he should ride home as quickly as possible. He believes that it was a miracle that he survived two attempts to shoot him at close range. He arrived home and greeted a terrified Freda, saying in disbelief to her, "They shot over me and tried to kill me!"

"Now will you stay home and listen to me!" was his wife's reply. Freda was very fearful for her husband's safety. His clerical collar (the white neck band worn by clergymen) was no longer a protection; rather, it marked him as a target. She had few friends with whom she could share, especially during the early days in their second parish because many of the church members were strict adherents to the reawakened movement and were suspicious of Freda. They treated her almost as an unbeliever. In due time Kolini and Freda won the love and respect of these people, and Freda found it hard to leave them when they moved to Congo.

At one time their home was very near the battle line between Amin's army and a group of Tanzanian Liberation Army soldiers who had come to help free the country from the dictator. One day a truckful of Amin's soldiers drove past their house and shouted, "We'll be back to visit you later!" They drove about three miles farther down the road and engaged in a battle. A gasoline tank was hit and exploded. It was like a bomb being dropped, and seventy soldiers were killed. A few of them managed to escape but were badly burned. Freda held her family close to her in their house and prayed. When the truck of soldiers passed by again, although they shot in the direction of their house, no one was hurt.

The Lord also spared them on another occasion. Freda had gone to bed but was awakened at ten o'clock by the noise of an army truck and the shouting of soldiers. The truck pulled up about 150 feet from their house, outside the primary school. Freda was sure that this time they intended to attack her family. With her children in bed with her, she committed them all to the Lord.

It happened to be Easter time, and at Easter and Christmas the children in the school had developed a custom of bringing to their teachers gifts of all kinds, including staples, vegetables, eggs, and even live chickens. These were then sold, and the money that was raised went to help the growing number of children orphaned by the Amin dictatorship. The soldiers broke into the school, saw all this food, and were delighted! They killed the chickens, lit fires, and cooked and ate the food. The enormous feast deflected them from their killing spree, and when they had finished eating, they drove away. Freda and the children remained safe and secure in the house; God was looking after them.

These were very difficult days for the people of Uganda, with rape and murder daily occurrences. Kolini recalls the sadness of constantly burying church members who had been victims of the violent regime. There was one particular month when he spent most of the time going from one little church to another, burying people. One day when they were burying a grandmother and her granddaughter together, the bishop was present and preached a sermon entitled "Lord, to Whom Else Can We Turn?" It was a real cry from the heart.

Indeed, people did turn to the Lord through this regime of terror, and despite all that was happening, the church grew and became stronger. Although all commodities were very scarce, the Christians found money and materials in order to build new churches and accommodate the growing number of converts. In Kampala it was reported that people were sleeping in the churches because they expected to be killed any day and would rather die praying in the house of God than anywhere else.

Before the liberation of Uganda and expulsion of Amin, a unit of his army was camped at Hoima, which was only eleven miles from Kolini's home. The intention was that all the prominent Christians in the area were to be killed. Kolini knew his bishop was on that list and was pretty sure it included his name as well. However, these murders did not occur because the liberation army attacked and killed about eighty of Amin's soldiers and the rest ran away. Kolini's parish was the frontline of this battle for three days. His family evacuated, grabbing blankets and cooking items, and lived in the bush for that time. Their house was burglarized and many things stolen, but God protected Kolini's books. These were his prize possessions, and he would have been devastated to lose them. At that time it would have been almost impossible to replace them. Neither did the soldiers touch the Communion elements, but they did steal his cassock (priest robe).

Amin was overthrown in 1979, and the end of that year marked change not only for Uganda, but also for the Kolini family.

CHAPTER 8

Reconnaissance Trip to Congo

The idea of moving to Congo had stayed with Kolini. In 1978 he had made a visit to Congo and met Bezareli Ndahura, the bishop of Bukavu. He had introduced himself as a Congolese who felt the call of God to return and work there.[1] The bishop had been very positive about the suggestion, and although he understood that Kolini was not yet free to leave his diocese in Uganda, the two men had agreed to keep in touch and had begun corresponding. Ndahura had also begun to communicate with Kolini's bishop, Yustasi Ruhindi, in Uganda.

In 1979 Kolini felt he could no longer resist the Lord's call back to his homeland. He knew in his heart it was time to resign from his parish and make preparations to return to Congo. He discussed it with his bishop and agreed to resign from the parish at the end of the year. He planned to go by himself the first of January 1980 to explore the possibilities of working there. It so happened that Archbishop Silvanus Wani from West Nile, Uganda, was also making a trip to Burundi via Rwanda, and Kolini was able to travel with him. It was better not to travel alone through these troubled countries at this time. As a Rwandan refugee, he was still barred from Rwanda, so when they stopped in Rwanda for meetings, Kolini didn't dare speak any Kinyarwanda for fear someone would guess he was Rwandan.

Freda was aware that her husband was feeling ever more strongly that he had a call to return to Congo, but she kept trying to keep the thoughts from her mind, and she had even tried to stop him from thinking and talking about it. Even after his resignation from the parish when he started to go around to the churches and say goodbye to people, Freda did not accompany him because in her mind it wasn't going to happen! She just couldn't believe that she was going to leave her home and travel to a foreign country far from her family and friends.

When January 1, 1980, dawned and Kolini had packed up his office and made preparations for his trip to Congo, her heart sank because she knew then that the move was inevitable. He said he would only be gone for a few weeks. When he left, Freda knew she had to prepare for the move and began harvesting the crops of sweet potatoes and peanuts from their garden to sell in the market. It was a very fertile piece of land that yielded a good harvest.

Then she began to sort their household belongings, getting rid of what they did not want or could not carry with them and packing the things they could take. By the end of the first week, she was prepared to move when Kolini returned. Freda also realized that there were changes in her body and that she must be pregnant again. With five children to feed and care for, they were already a large family.

The weeks went by, and there was no news of Kolini. The waiting stretched into a month. Some of the church members realized that every day must be difficult for her and the children since all their belongings were packed, and they came to visit Freda. One family said to her, "Don't worry; you can share our house until he returns. We love our pastor so much; maybe he has changed his mind and will come back to us!" They offered her two rooms in their house so she and the children would be protected until Kolini returned. It was a tight squeeze for them to live in just two rooms, but Freda was grateful for the love and friendship shown to her at that difficult time.

One month dragged into two, and still there was no word from Kolini. Freda had taken her children out of school for the move, and now the long school holidays were over. The headmaster came to visit her and suggested that the children go back to school for the time being and even provided uniforms for them to wear. The headmaster and so many parishioners, expressed their secret hope that Kolini would return and remain with them. He was greatly beloved as their pastor, and they did not want to lose him. While he had been pastor, the church had flourished financially and in membership. It was hard to think that these were the same people who had made life so difficult for them in the early days in the parish. These people had been completely won over by Kolini and Freda's love and understanding.

Two and a half months had passed, and Freda was very concerned about the lack of news from Kolini. She was pregnant, had five other children to support, had no income, and had no idea what had happened to her husband. Although Idi Amin had been deposed, Uganda, like Congo, was still a volatile country. There was always the possibility of bandits as well as threats from disease and wild animals. Freda felt that perhaps she ought to leave the parish and return to Kinyara camp where both sets of parents were living. She had been asking the Lord what she should do and felt this was his answer and decided to discuss her plans with the bishop. He welcomed her and listened intently while she shared her predicament with him. As they were talking together, he received a telephone call.

Missing, Presumed Dead

The phone call was, in fact, a message about Kolini. The caller asked if Kolini had arrived back in Hoima yet. The bishop replied that no one had heard from Kolini for almost three months. The caller reported that Kolini had been seen in Kampala three days before and had left in a Land Rover to return to Hoima. It was feared that he had been ambushed and robbed of the large amount of money he was carrying with him. The caller suggested that a search party be sent out to find his body.

The bishop decided that the kindest thing to do was to withhold the news until they had recovered Kolini's body. He came back and told Freda that he agreed with her decision to go back to her parents but suggested she wait for another day or two. The bishop would send his car to pick up the family, and then they would travel on to Kinyara camp.

Freda returned home without suspecting anything was amiss. Early the next day, just as the bishop had promised, he sent his car to get them. When they arrived in Hoima, eleven miles away, they stopped in the town center, where a group of women had arranged to meet her and the children. However, Freda had arrived earlier than expected and had quickly arranged transport to the camp. Among the group of women was Harriet, the wife of John Rucyahana, their close friend. These women had been asked to take care of Freda, but since Kolini's body had not been found, they decided to protect her from the news. Freda was both mystified and bewildered by all the attention but decided that it meant nothing in particular and boarded the hired vehicle to take her to the camp.

The bishop's intention was to have the family stay in his home overnight and to talk to Freda before she returned to her parents' home. However, in ignorance of the bishop's plan, she was on her way back to the refugee camp. Harriet went with her, but that was no surprise to Freda because John and Harriet lived near the camp. What was a surprise, though, was that Harriet continued to stay with the family when they finally arrived at her parents' home.

Over the next day or so, Freda kept wondering why Harriet was just sitting with her and not even talking very much. She thought, "Doesn't Harriet have a home to go back to or work to do? Why isn't she going back to cook for her children?" It just didn't make sense. An uneasy silence hung heavily between them, unspoken words that one woman didn't want to say and the other didn't dare ask. Freda wondered what was going on.

On Saturday her mother suggested that she take the children to visit their paternal grandparents, as they would want to spend time with them also. Freda agreed and took the family to Kolini's parents, where they stayed for the next week. Toward the end of the week, Freda had a conversation with her mother-in-law that shocked her. Kolini's mother had decided that she would go to Bukavu to try to find out what had happened to her son. Her plan was to go first to Kampala, where John Rucyahana was studying, and make inquiries. If she could not find any information, she would travel to Congo. She said that if she did not find him in Bukavu, then she would not return but would just disappear and live in the bush in Congo. She did not want to take care of all the family if he was dead.

Freda was disturbed by this conversation. What was her mother-in-law really thinking? All the tensions of the past weeks had been too much, and Freda broke down and wept. "If you go and don't come back, how will I manage?" she sobbed.

About nine o'clock that evening, Freda and her mother-in-law were sitting outside the house in the moonlight. They were able to see quite well on such a moonlit night, and they spotted a car driving very slowly around the camp. It stopped outside the home of Freda's parents. It was strange for a car to be around at that time of night. They wondered what was going on. Was someone asking for food? After a while, the car started up again and came slowly around the camp to their area.

People appeared from nowhere and, in the gathering excitement, began to chant, "Kolini! Kolini! Kolini!" Could it be? Was it true? Had Kolini finally arrived home? There was a large crowd, including Harriet, who had braved walking through the bush even though there was a danger from wild animals. Freda thought Harriet was beside herself with excitement, and she didn't understand why. "What is wrong?" she asked her.

"Didn't you hear the story?" Harriet replied. "Has nobody told you? Let me tell you. We all heard that Kolini was dead. It was the phone call the day you visited the bishop to tell him you had decided to go home."

No wonder everyone had acted so strangely. When all the fuss had calmed down and people had returned to their homes, Freda and Kolini were able to talk together about what had been happening through the months they had been separated. He told her that when they had arrived in Burundi, the Congolese border closed, and he had no way of letting her know that he was delayed. The border finally opened two months later, and he was able to travel with a Congolese bishop to Bukavu, the Congolese border town.

When he did eventually get into Congo, he had used his time, while waiting for his papers, not only to prepare for relocating his family but also to brush up on both his French and his Swahili. He had become a bit rusty in these languages while living in Uganda and using English a great deal. When he got new papers as a Congolese citizen, he was able to go back to Burundi for meetings with the Rwandans and act as interpreter. He could understand everything that was being said in Kinyarwanda and interpret it to the Congolese. There were difficulties between the Rwandans and the Congolese, and Burundi was the buffer state. The whole trip had been extended much longer than he had anticipated.

The following day they went to Hoima to collect their belongings from storage, and the family, plus Kolini's parents, all squeezed into one car and set off overland to Congo. Because there had been no time to obtain travel documents for the whole family, it had been arranged that the local priest would meet them near the border with members of his congregation. They would escort Freda and all the rest of the family and carry their belongings through the bush into Congo. The driver and Kolini, who did have papers, went through the Rutshuru-Ishasha border crossing. Then they met up with the family again and continued their journey.

CHAPTER 9

Congo at Last

S o began a new chapter of their lives as they started work and ministry in Bukavu. Life was initially very hard for the family, and Freda and Kolini decided to leave two of their children, Christopher and John, with his parents—who were staying at his uncle's house near the border—until they had a home where they could take care of them.

Freda found the move to Congo a real culture shock. She didn't speak Swahili, and she couldn't understand the money, making each visit to the market quite an adventure. The family had been allocated a very small house, but they had no furniture. They put mattresses on the floor each night when they went to bed, but it was not very comfortable for Freda, who was five months pregnant. They were not given any salary, so finding enough food for the family was a real problem. Freda lost so much weight that one old man of their acquaintance became very concerned for her. Fortunately, her "baby bump" was still growing.

On September 7, 1980, after only nine months in Bukavu as a parish priest, Kolini was consecrated as assistant bishop to Archbishop Bezareli Ndahura. He was just thirty-five years old. At that time the primacy was made up of the three Francophone countries of Congo, Rwanda, and Burundi, and Bezareli Ndahura was the first primate of the province. The archbishop was also a bishop of a diocese that covered half of Congo, so he was in great need of someone to help him. He worked tirelessly to spread the gospel in Congo with very few resources. The church grew in an amazing way under his leadership, and he was a great role model and inspiration to Kolini.

In his new ministry in Congo, Kolini soon realized that he needed a different approach to the way he cared for his flock. The Ugandans, most of whom had been refugees, had needed a gentle approach, but he found he needed to be far more direct in the way he spoke to people in Congo. It was difficult for him to use strong words when talking to people, but that was the language the people understood and to which they responded best. The needs of his parish were totally different, Bukavu being a large town, as opposed to a rural, refugee community with few facilities.

The diocese was newly formed and so lacked both personnel and finances. There was no allowance for Kolini, and his family often went hungry. Freda considered going to stay with Kolini's parents for a short time. Harry had been complaining that he would not go to bed without food, and often they had only a cup of tea to give the children. However, Freda realized if she did this, her actions could easily be misconstrued as family problems. To leave was not the wisest solution. For a month Kolini formed a habit of disappearing in the evenings, and Freda wondered where he had gone. When she asked her husband, she learned that he had been in the chapel, interceding with the Lord to come and rescue them.

The time came for Freda's baby to be delivered, and she went to the local hospital. As was the custom in Congo, the patient's family had to provide the meals, either bringing meals from home each mealtime or staying and cooking them outside the hospital. There was so little food that could be brought to Freda, and what there was had little nutritional value. She found it very hard to eat it without vomiting. However, Freda safely delivered her seventh child, David, but was far from well afterward. Kolini was in a dilemma because he was due to go on a ministry tour that would take him hundreds of miles away to Beni for confirmations and from there on a nine-hour bicycle ride into the Rwenzori Mountains to confirm five hundred candidates and give Communion to eight hundred people.

He went to the hospital and requested that Freda be discharged so that she could be at home with the children during his trip. The doctor refused, thinking that Freda was not well enough and needed at least one more day of care. Although he was reluctant to do so, Kolini decided that he would have to sign discharge papers for his wife and take her home against medical advice. That night Freda became increasingly sick. She was very weak and her body shook. Kolini covered her with his cassock while she shivered. It wrenched his heart to leave her like that, not only with the tiny baby but also with all the other children to care for. But Freda reminded him that the Lord had protected them through many crises over the years and that he wouldn't desert them now. So Kolini went to Beni, and somehow Freda managed to regain her strength.

This proved to be a very arduous trip for him. It rained hard, and he had to ford the river while carrying his bicycle on his shoulders. He returned from that trip at six o'clock in the morning, having traveled by car all through the night. He freshened up, picked up his bag, and was whisked off in the car for important meetings in Burundi. For this couple, in their devotion to God, life meant sacrifice and courage.

While Kolini was away on one of his long trips as assistant bishop, baby David became ill. He woke up one morning and cried incessantly; nothing Freda did could pacify him. He did not even want to be nursed. She looked carefully at her little son and saw that the left side of his face and jaw was very swollen. She could not see any mark to indicate that he had been bitten, and she had no idea what might have caused the problem, but it was obvious that something was seriously wrong with David. She picked him up and ran outside to try to get help. Seeing the wife of the archbishop on the porch of her house, she asked her to come and look at David. Mama Suez thought perhaps it was a bite of some sort and told Freda to go to the dispensary. Freda had to tell her that she had no money, and all treatment had to be paid for in advance.

Mama Suez wrote a note asking them to treat the baby and defer payment until it was available, which they did, but no one at the dispensary knew how to help him. The medicine they gave David didn't relieve his symptoms, and he continued to worsen. Freda was desperate and decided, even though she had no money, that she must take David at once to the hospital. When she arrived and the doctor saw the condition of the baby, he admitted him at once, asking no questions about payment. Freda stayed in the hospital with David to nurse and care for him. The hospital staff brought her some food, but she was too worried about her other little ones at home to eat much. In utter misery, one day she sat outside on the grass, looking over Lake Kivu, and cried out to the Lord to bring her husband home. The Lord heard the cry of his daughter and had mercy on her in that desperate situation.

Kolini arrived back at Bukavu later that day and found that his wife and baby had been in the hospital almost a week. They never discovered what had made David so sick, but thankfully he made an almost complete recovery, except for some slight hearing loss that became permanent.

The financial situation continued to be dire, and Kolini and Freda cried out constantly to the Lord to rescue them and meet their needs. The answer came in due course. Christopher Carey, the regional secretary of the Anglican Church Mission Society (CMS)[1], paid a visit to Congo, and Kolini and Freda had opportunity to share their situation with him. When he returned to England, he was able to tell people in supporting churches of the need of this family, and one parish decided to send a sacrificial gift of four hundred British pounds (a great deal of money at the time) to the Kolini family. It came just as they were being required to move to the Shaba district and was a wonderful provision that enabled Freda to stay with her husband rather than return to her family.

The dioceses of the Anglican Church in Congo were huge and almost impossible to administer or pastor. The synod decided to create three new dioceses and make Kolini the bishop of one of these. When Freda heard the news—even though she had not visited any of the three places—her heart leaped when she heard the name of Shaba. This was one of the suggested places for the new bishop to be based, and in her spirit Freda knew that this was where the Lord wanted them to go. Of the three new proposed sees, it was the least likely placement for Kolini. But quietly and confidently, Freda kept on praying. Although everyone else was surprised when he was appointed as the bishop of Shaba, she was not. The Shaba district was later renamed Katanga, and the cathedral was at Lubumbashi, previously called Elizabethville.

CHAPTER 10

Ministry at Shaba

The family once again packed up their few possessions and started the six-hour journey by boat, followed by a one-hour flight, to their new home. At least, it should have been their new home, but there was no welcome committee, no red carpet, not even a house for them. The priest provided two rooms for the family to squeeze into for the two weeks it took to find a house. The house they found was in dire need of painting, so for a while the family moved from room to room, heaving mattresses around while different rooms were duly painted. It was six months before they were able to purchase some furniture and could settle in properly.

A month after Kolini's appointment and move to Shaba, Archbishop Bezareli Ndahura died, and a time of very difficult church politics ensued. Once again Kolini found that he was regarded as a foreigner, much as he had been in Uganda.

Finances

The new diocese had no personnel and no finances. For three years there was no salary for Kolini; it was two and a half years before he even had a bicycle to ride. The Lord provided help through a missionary who wrote to his mission's head office in New York, asking if they would support Kolini on a regular basis so that he could maintain his work. They agreed, but the money had to go to a bank three thousand miles away in Rwanda, as banks were no longer operative in Bukavu. The money was then changed into Congo currency and sent to the diocese before it was sent to Kolini. The diocese kept half the money in Bukavu for its own use.

Kolini challenged the diocese about this transaction because all the money should have been sent for his support as it was intended. The treasurer for the Shaba diocese was an Englishman, John Hayward, and he understood the problem and wrote to the mission in New York, asking them to send the money directly to Kolini. A bank account was opened for Kolini in New York, and then he was able to receive a regular allowance. The family was supported in this way for three years, with John Hayward also supplementing them from his own pocket.

Kolini refers to this part of his life as "the days in the desert with Jesus." As in Genesis 21 when God provided Hagar a source of fresh water in the desert, this was God's provision for Kolini and his family. The times in Uganda when he was a teacher and then as a priest, followed by the times in Congo, were difficult, but the lessons learned prepared him for what was yet to come in Rwanda. He says of those times, "You have to go through fire in order to face up to such a situation as this [meaning Rwanda]. Of course, the Lord leads you to do it; otherwise, you can't survive. Those were the days of hardship, but they were also the days of the Lion God. Those are the days you trust in God! It was like the days of Elijah when he was fed by the ravens!" For him, the greatest lesson of all was listening to what the Lord was saying.

His theological training could not have prepared him for all he would face. President Mobutu had outlawed the independent churches because he was afraid that they would form political parties and oppose him. Since the Anglican Church was a recognized church and allowed by Mobutu, many people joined it. There was a huge influx into Kolini's church at Shaba of about three thousand people who had left their independent churches. These new people had no understanding of the Anglican Church, so he was sent to teach them. The young bishop had to deal with people from many different backgrounds who, often, were nominal Christians. They were struggling in every way—politically, socially, and economically. They needed help and they needed answers. They had come from different church backgrounds into the Anglican Church, and many were still searching for God. If he could not meet their spiritual needs, they might become spiritual nomads, wandering from church to church and never finding Christ, never being satisfied.

The Shaba cathedral had previously been St. Andrew's chaplaincy for the expatriate community in Lubumbashi. It had been started to serve the many English and Zambian people who lived there in the heyday of the railway, which used to run from South Africa to Elizabethville (Lubumbashi). There continued to be one service at Shaba cathedral for a small group of expatriates. This was a group of about fifty members, mostly Zambian. Over ten years this congregation grew to number more than ten thousand.

One of these members was an engineer named Eric, who worked in a soap factory. This man proved to be a blessing to the family while they were living in these difficult circumstances. The diocese had managed to buy two small houses and a houseboy's quarters, but that was all the senior bishop could do for the new bishop. The Kolini family had no salary, no transportation, and no way of supporting itself. The soap factory in Lubumbashi for which Eric worked was relocating, and he helped the Kolini family buy furniture that was no longer needed by the factory. Again, it was a time of seeing again the goodness of God as their heavenly Father.

Another person the Lord used to provide for the family was a missionary named Tylor, who shared his mission allowance with them. But transportation remained a problem; it was difficult to travel around a diocese that was as large as the country of Kenya. Kolini used public transportation when he could, such as the train, riding in a primitive railcar that had no windows or bed. Sometimes he had to travel miles on foot, but there were always dangers from the unsettled political situation, wild animals, fast-flowing rivers, and many other obstacles that could discourage even the most intrepid of travelers.

One night their son John became very ill. Everyone is fearful when sickness strikes in Central and East Africa because of the swiftness with which it can terminate a life. Kolini and Freda were extremely worried about their small son John. He needed help quickly, and it was well over half a mile to the hospital. There was no public transportation at one o'clock in the morning. There was only one option, and that was to carry him to the hospital; they arrived in time for John to be successfully treated.

This incident highlighted the great need that Kolini had for some sort of transportation of his own. Tylor felt that he should help the situation and bought a motorbike for Kolini. The very day he purchased it, John became ill again—at three in the morning. But this time Kolini was able to get him to hospital in just a matter of minutes. How grateful they were for the kindness of this young missionary.

When Tylor's parents came to visit him, they were able to hand-carry letters to Europe for their son, letters that he wrote to some of his friends to tell about Kolini's situation. It was difficult to communicate easily in the 1970s in Congo before the era of computers, e-mails, and cell phones; and the mail was slow and unreliable, so it was a real benefit to send letters with someone.

Tylor told his friends and prayer partners about the lack of transportation, and they were able to raise enough money for the purchase of a small car that had belonged to a Rwandan refugee who had been a soldier in Amin's army in Uganda. This served Kolini for a while, and when he needed to replace it, enough funds were provided to buy a new car—a Toyota. It was shipped from Japan to Mombasa in Kenya and then had to be driven to

Congo. The car arrived eighteen months later, making life much easier.

Before when he used to walk the long distances to visit people and churches, he had to put his cross into his pocket so it would not bang against his chest, but when he was able to drive, he noticed that he could wear it around his neck once again. It was just a small thing, but very significant to him at the time as a reminder of the Lord's care.

Traveling in Congo

When the small car arrived, it was an enormous blessing, even though travel was still far from easy, especially on the poorly maintained roads. Most of the roads were of red laterite earth, which in the rainy season turned into a sea of mud with very deep potholes. In the dry season the surface was deeply rutted and shook every bone in the body. It was easy to skid on the dried-out surface, and whenever another vehicle approached, everybody's vision was obscured by clouds of fine red dust. At the end of a journey, travelers looked like some sort of strange aliens covered in dust. The first thing to offer a guest was a tub of water.

Kolini never knew what would happen on a trip. One time when the family was traveling, they came to a river with a small and very rickety bridge over it. It didn't look very safe, so the family got out and walked across and then tried to guide Kolini as he drove on to the narrow planks. He was about three-quarters over the bridge, driving very cautiously, when he heard a crack, and the whole structure began to give way. Caution went to the wind, and he put the vehicle into gear and almost made it leap, safely arriving on the other side just before the bridge fell into the river. Incidents like this were only too common on Congo roads. This event meant they could not travel home the same way. The detour took four extra days and put them at risk of running out of fuel.

Another time Kolini and Freda were traveling with three other adults and two small children in the car. They were on a six-day trip and needed to cross the Congo River. When they arrived at a ferry point, they found that the ferry was on the opposite bank. It was late afternoon, and because there was no car on that side to bring over, the ferry did not come. Although it was hard to understand why the ferry would not come to take them across since it was not yet really dark, the travelers were not too daunted by this. In the car were safari beds and supplies, so they decided to camp on the riverbank for the night. They lit a fire and made themselves as comfortable as possible, sleeping under the stars.

After a while, when they had all gone to sleep, it started to rain. When it rains in the tropics, it is not the gentle, soft rain; the heavens open and it pours. Everyone can be drenched in seconds. The group hastily packed up the camping things and piled back into the car, trying somehow to get comfortable enough to get a few moments of sleep. When morning dawned, to their relief the ferry, carrying another vehicle, arrived. They finally understood the delay: the ferry had no battery to drive its engine and expected the car driver to remove his battery for the ferry to use to cross the river. The travelers eventually arrived safely on the other side of the river.

Times of Fellowship

Kolini enjoyed fellowship with others in the service of ministry. His years in Uganda had given him experiences of fellowship in the *balokole* movement, where, especially in the refugee camp, they had enjoyed wonderful times, meeting together and "walking in the light" with each other. When the family returned to Congo, there was no such fellowship, and Kolini and Freda felt spiritually lonely among the Congolese. They found that their hunger for fellowship was often satisfied only when they met together with the missionaries in the area who were from various denominations. On Sunday evenings they would all try to meet together. At first some of the missionaries, especially from the Brethren missions, were a little unsure of welcoming an Anglican bishop into their homes and eventually admitted they thought he probably would not be a true believer. How wrong they were. The friendships grew, and these missionaries were supportive and encouraging to Kolini and Freda.

There were some young volunteer missionaries who often came to their home in the early days at Shaba, before the Kolini family had any transportation of their own. These young missionaries became members of the family and always called Freda "Mom." The Congolese were amazed at this and teased her that she must also have a *muzungu* husband hidden somewhere. These adopted children helped her in the home, even looking after the children as their own younger brothers and sisters. They also helped out with transportation whenever they could and brought much joy, laughter, and fellowship to Freda, Kolini, and the children.

Through the years the links remained with many of the missionaries from the independent churches and also from the indigenous churches, although there were some of the latter group who became envious when Kolini was given a World Vision vehicle for his ministry. He tried to counteract this by generously giving rides to others whenever he was able. Some of the indigenous churches also felt that all robes used by clergymen were a curse rather than a blessing, and because of this they did not want to associate with ministers from the Anglican Church (even though Kolini only wore his robes for special occasions such as Christmas, Easter, and ordinations).

In time Kolini became "bishop" to many of the foreign missionaries from other denominations, and they came to him to ask for prayer and to discuss the problems they were experiencing in leadership.

New Groups Joining the Church

In 1990 a whole group of believers who belonged to the Pentecostal church came to him, wishing to become Anglicans. They had one problem, they explained, and that was, as they understood, the Anglican Church was not a Spirit-filled church. But they looked at the Anglicans and saw a stability that their church lacked and for which they longed. The Pentecostals seemed to be constantly on the move, leaving one congregation to join another; there was nothing like the settled parish life that they saw in the Anglican Church. Also, there were no schools or clinics or other services for their families. As they talked with Kolini about both their needs and their concerns, he prayed and asked the Lord how he could help these brethren.

Kolini then decided he could run a seminar for these people in order to help them understand more about the beliefs of the Anglican Church. So he convened a two-week seminar for his own churches and invited the Pentecostals to come and explore the faith and beliefs of the Anglicans.

Kolini asked them how they had heard the gospel. They told him that they had heard it while living in Burundi. "Well," replied Kolini, "the Pentecostal church in Burundi grew out of the East African Revival, which sprang initially from the Anglican Church!" This group of believers was amazed and relieved when they heard that. They listened for two weeks as Kolini preached and discussed issues with them. At the end of the two weeks he asked them what they thought, and they decided to join the Anglican Church. Their questions had been answered and their fears allayed. Five parish churches sprang from these Pentecostal groups.

Kolini remarks that the Anglicans were blessed by them as much as they were blessed by joining the Anglican Church. It was interesting that these people grew to love the prayer book they had previously despised, and their ministers began to enjoy wearing a cassock, surplice, and scarf.

The first Communion service with them was another matter because they objected to being given wine. In their churches they had used Coca-Cola, believing that drinking any alcohol was a sin. Kolini explained that not only did our Lord use wine, but it was far more hygienic as it killed, rather than bred, germs.

Also the silver chalice was cleaner and safer to drink from than the cracked local cups. The chalice was expensive and so was washed and polished carefully after each use, whereas ordinary household items, especially in the villages, were not always taken care of. Once they had tasted the wine, they dropped all their objections. As they drank it and felt it warm them inside, they felt it was the Holy Spirit touching them. Because wine was so expensive, the wafer was just dipped into the wine for most parishioners, but the pastors of these new churches and their wives requested to be given the wine from the cup. It brought great joy to Kolini to see these brethren accepting both the prayer book and also the wine as a eucharistic element.

Education

Kolini always had a burden for education, beginning when he had started the school in the refugee camp in Uganda. Wherever he worked, he was interested in starting new church schools and also concerned to improve existing ones. In the Shaba area he oversaw the beginnings of twenty-two schools—fourteen primary and eight secondary. One of these secondary schools in the city started with 120 pupils and grew to 1,200.

In the schools Kolini endorsed two basic rules: discipline and good management. The people were very poor and unable to afford much for school fees. The little that was charged was well managed, so the schools were viable. Some of the schools were in the slums, where poverty was extreme and the children had previously been denied any realistic hope of an education. The good management rules made it possible for schools to blossom even in this environment. They became strong and survived at a time when the government schools were collapsing. The Catholics came and begged him to take their children into one of his schools. Kolini explained to them that the problem was they had run out of desks for children to use. The Catholics said they would supply the necessary desks. That is indeed what happened, and the Catholic children were welcomed. The Anglican schools thrived. Kolini's own children attended the local church school, and he would check on the teachers and the administration regularly.

Church Matters

These early years as a bishop were times of learning for Kolini. He was still a young man and had to learn to be flexible, which is sometimes hard to learn at a young age. Although he wanted everything to be done in an orderly and, perhaps, traditional Anglican way, he realized that some of the Anglican traditions were a stumbling block to his new flock, especially to those who had come to join the church from other church traditions.

The wearing of vestments and even, for a short while, the use of the prayer book had to be discarded because they were hindering the gospel. For the ex-Catholics, the wearing of robes reminded them of the Catholic priests who were associated with the colonial era, bringing memories to the people of the wrong use of power and its corruption. They had left the church because they were so unhappy with the church's involvement in the colonial government. They did not want to be part of a church that constantly reminded them of colonial times and oppression. There were many ex-Catholics in their churches because Congo had been predominately Roman Catholic under Belgian rule.

Kolini did not want anything to hinder these people from coming to church and meeting the Lord, so he was happy not to have vestments worn in the churches. The Methodists wore cassocks, and the congregations were used to these and found them acceptable. So they were quite content for Kolini to wear a cassock when leading worship.

Those who had joined the flock from the independent churches did not understand the use of a prayer book and were upset with a written form of service and prayers. Kolini sat down with the leaders, showed them a prayer book, and asked them what they saw. They were amazed to see quotations from the Bible. Kolini told them, "You cannot accept the hymnbook and reject the prayer book because they all come from the Bible."

So within a short time, the prayer book was accepted and used in the churches. In the course of time, some of the leaders of the independent church went to Anglican Church members to borrow their prayer books so they could make copies of services, such as marriage and burial, because they didn't know how to conduct these services.

Another situation that the young bishop felt he needed to address was to change the entry rules to join the Mothers' Union.[1] This movement had a strict rule that only married women could belong. In Congo many couples had never had a church blessing on their marriage, even some of the pastors. Were they to be excluded? Because the Mothers' Union was a very strong and evangelistic tool for spreading the gospel, by discarding this rule, their branches grew stronger and the Lord blessed them.

So Kolini learned to be flexible by listening to God; he didn't want anything to be a barrier to people coming to know God. He did as the apostle Paul wrote in 1 Corinthians 9:22: "To the weak I became weak, to win the weak. I have become all things to all men so that by all possible means I might save some." He had to learn where he could not compromise and where he could let things go. In this way the church grew.

Training Leaders

Not only was Kolini being taught to be strong as a leader, but he was also learning that it can be very lonely at the top of the ladder and, therefore, how important it is to recognize leadership qualities in others and to help them fulfill their potential. Because his clergy needed to be helped forward as much as possible, their education became another priority. Theological Education by Extension (TEE)[2] was becoming available in Congo, but nobody had any books. Each time Kolini made a trip to Bukavu, he would buy a book to put on his bookshelf. His students would borrow these books and take them to their rural parishes out in the bush because they had no reference material and had not previously been given any theological teaching or training at all.

First Ordinations

After a while Kolini was able to conduct his first ordinations. He bought some material and arranged for cassocks and scarves to be made for his new deacons—and they loved them. So gradually the churches became accustomed to their pastors being robed in cassocks. Kolini himself put his full robes on only at Christmas, Easter, and for ordinations. The rest of the time he wore his purple cassock, and this helped to break down the prejudices and barriers.

The need for additional theological training also became apparent, so he asked the Africa Evangelistic Enterprise (AEE)[3] in Nairobi if they would be willing to do some training in Congo. Pleased to help, they came initially for a month and conducted evangelistic campaigns in two provinces. Then for three years they organized yearly seminars, helping both the lay leaders and parish priests to learn how to evangelize and spiritually lead in their parishes. Kolini also invited leaders from other denominations to attend. As they began to learn more about the Anglican Church, some additional barriers were broken down. In this way the whole church in Congo benefited and grew stronger. It also gave the Anglican pastors a sense of confidence when they came into the diocese for these conferences, helping them to know where they belonged. They were not just out in the bush running a church on their own, but belonged to a much bigger fellowship, both nationally and internationally.

Freda was also a leader and headed up the Mothers' Union. World Vision gave a three-year grant for a program teaching hygiene, nutrition, and other related subjects. It helped to bring

Christian values into the Congolese culture where women were marginalized. After church services on Sundays, special meetings were organized in which the men and women could talk together and ask questions about marriage and family life. This was a revolutionary idea at that time in Congo's history.

On one occasion Kolini was visiting a church and asked the priest how the program was being received. The priest complained rather bitterly that each week when the meeting convened, he spent all his time listening to his parishioners' marital problems. Kolini explained to him the importance of marriage and family life in the church and society and that the wife has a pivotal place in the center of the home. She stands between the husband and the children. She is the one who is at home and cares for the children while the husband is usually the one who is away as the breadwinner. The wife takes the hand of the child and the hand of the father, bringing them together. Kolini told his priest that he saw the wife as the center of a stable home, and that is why he so encouraged the World Vision program and thought such teaching was valuable and badly needed to strengthen Congolese society.

Other programs that were developed to strengthen the church during this time were the Boys' Brigade[4] and the American Fellowship of the Brotherhood of St. Andrew.[5] These groups were successful in capturing the interest of the men and boys and helped significantly in spreading the gospel among the unevangelized within the diocese.

There had been a time when the late Right Reverend Yustasi Rukindi, former bishop of Bunyoro, Kitara, and then later bishop of Rukungiri, had counseled Kolini: "If you don't prepare a Timothy or Joshua, then you will have failed in your ministry." So that is what he tried to do, making disciples and training future leaders for the church.

Because of these strong groups—the Mothers' Union, the Boys' Brigade, the Brotherhood, and the lay ministry—when things became difficult in later years and Kolini's successor was away, the diocese still stood firm until he returned.

The emphasis in the diocese was not only to train leaders but also to reach the next generation, to build the church of the future. The Boys' Brigade was a great tool for this, and when President Kabila visited Shaba district, the Brigade's companies paraded before him, about eight hundred boys all proudly wearing their uniforms. One of the pastors was their commanding officer and stood commanding them right in front of the president. It was a great advertisement for the church and the work it was doing among the youth. President Kabila was very impressed.

Looking back, Kolini thanks God for all that was established in the ministry in Congo, but it was at a considerable cost. It meant being away from home a great deal and traveling long distances under very difficult circumstances. He and Freda constantly proved that the Lord was with them as their protector and deliverer.

In the late 1980s CMS sent two couples to help Kolini in his work. Tim and Hilary Naish were from England and Steve and Kathy Ross were from New Zealand. It was so good to have reinforcements.

Tim oversaw the TEE program, and Steve was a medical doctor. Tim was a deacon when he went to Congo as a missionary, and while he was there, Kolini ordained him as a priest. These couples have good memories of their time working in the diocese of Shaba. Both couples now live and work in the Oxford area of England. Steve is a general practitioner and his wife works for CMS. Tim is a priest serving on a theological faculty within Oxford University. Even now the couples meet together in England: they share fond memories of their time working alongside Kolini in Congo.

The archbishop who was over the province of the Francophone countries of Congo, Burundi, and Rwanda was based at Bukavu, Congo. One time Kolini was visiting with him when President Mobutu of Congo was also in the Bukavu area. They were able to meet him and discuss the possibility of the Anglican Church being independent in the same way that the Catholic Church, the Orthodox Church, and the Muslims were. There were fifty-two registered Protestant church groups, but they were all treated as one group and labeled as independent churches. The Anglicans wanted to be acknowledged and respected for who they are. Although the president seemed very favorable to their request, the head of the Protestant council was opposed to it. As a result, while he was in office, Anglicans were denied independence, and their leaders were persecuted for the next six years by their fellow Protestants.

Other Protestant groups were watching carefully because they also wanted to leave the council and be free of the government restrictions. The request of the Anglicans was threatening the break up of the Protestant Council of Congo. A compromise was reached in which the Anglicans were no longer treated as an independent church. Following this resolution, Kolini became the moderator of the Protestant churches in his area for five years. He was mostly required to reconcile conflicts among the various churches. This made Kolini realize once more the desperate need for leadership and theological training in the area for all Protestant denominations, so he instituted Bible colleges in Lubumbashi and Kasai (Kananga).

After 1980 Kolini was able to return to Rwanda for provincial meetings. He had become cofounder of AEE in Rwanda and needed to visit the country for administrative purposes. His involvement with the starting of AEE in Rwanda had come about when he was attending a training seminar for new bishops in Nairobi and discussed with Ugandan Bishop Festo Kivengere the need and possibility to set up some training in Rwanda. That led to the establishment of an AEE office in Kigali. AEE had wanted to establish an office in Burundi, but permission was refused. A national team leader was appointed—Israel Harugimana. He was a godly man, an outspoken defender of the gospel. Although a Hutu, he was killed on the first day of the 1994 genocide and was the first Anglican martyr of that conflict.

CHAPTER 11

Rwanda's Dark History

T he ethnic hatred that erupted into genocide in 1994 had its roots many years earlier in the colonial era. Historically, the three racial groups had lived side by side in reasonable harmony for many hundreds of years before the Europeans invaded the land. The ruling group was the Batutsi.

After Germany's defeat in World War I and the Belgian government became the new colonial power, there was a deliberate political policy to undermine the authority of the *mwami*. So in 1931 the king was forced to abdicate in favor of his son, Mutara Rudahigwa. Once enthroned, the new *mwami* became nothing more than a puppet ruler. He became westernized in his outlook, converted to Roman Catholicism, and lived in a palace built for him by the Belgians in Nyanza. He began to lobby for independence from Belgian rule, with the intention of reinstating the power of the Tutsi kingdom. On July 24, 1959, Rudahigwa died in mysterious circumstances in Usumbura (later known as Bujumbura), the capital of Burundi. No explanation was ever given as to the manner or cause of his death. As he died without a successor, Jean-Baptist Ndahindurwa was appointed as the new Mwami Kigeri V, following the traditional Rwandese process and without any consultation with the Belgian authorities.

There is no clear evidence of who initiated these political moves, but very soon after his installation, there were a number of brutal political assassinations of prominent Hutu men. Terrible reprisals followed as the Hutu rose up against the Tutsi, killing not just those in public positions of leadership but many thousands of people across the country. During this wave of racial violence, it is estimated that around 12,000 Tutsi and moderate Hutu were killed, and over 100,000 fled as refugees into Uganda, Tanzania, Congo, and Burundi.

This bloodshed was a great challenge to both the Anglican Church leaders and the missionaries. The church had within its leadership both Tutsi priests and Hutu priests. Mission stations quickly became refugee centers, and the countryside became the scene of burned houses and vandalized banana and coffee plantations. When terror-stricken Tutsi fled to missionary homes for protection, sometimes those within the church as well as many outside looked on their protection as being politically pro-Tutsi.

In 1962 the Belgium government granted independence to Rwanda, but, sadly, the departure of the Belgians did not end the hatred and violence. Seeds of genocide were already planted, and extremist Hutu wanted to see the Tutsi gone forever from the land. The refugees wanted justice, so insurgent raids began from over the borders into Rwanda. They were only successful in stirring up more hatred and reprisals against the Tutsi who had remained in the land. A massacre ensued of another 10,000 Tutsi.

Yona's Story

At Nyamata, the main town of the Bugesera region, the situation became very tense in the latter months of 1963. Just outside Nyamata is the Anglican center of Maranyundo, and the priest there was Yona Kanamuzeyi. Yona had been one of the schoolboys at Gahini when the revival had been at its height, and he had experienced the power of God touching his life. He had been a faithful servant of God ever since those days. In the renewed outbreak of violence in Bugesera, the government soldiers were intimidating and exterminating anyone they thought might be aiding Tutsi insurgents who were crossing the borders from the refugee camps.

Yona was a man of God, living his life with his wife, Mary, and serving his parish. He had no involvement in politics, and in fact no one seems to know whether he was a Tutsi or a Hutu. It just wasn't an issue. He was a pastor with a loving heart, caring for all who came to him for help. This infuriated the government anti-Tutsi soldiers.

The text of his sermon on Sunday, January 19, 1964, was Romans 6:4: "We were therefore buried with him through baptism into death in order that, just as Christ was raised from the dead through the glory of the Father, we too may live a new life." Yona knew what it was like to experience that new life through the death of Christ.

By January 23 Yona had received information that his name was on a list of wanted men. Such men were usually taken from their homes at gunpoint during the night and never seen alive again. The night air would often ring with the sound of gunshots.

That January day Yona had a visit from Ian Leakey, a senior missionary friend. They talked together about the situation and then spent a time of prayer together. Ian recalls that Yona prayed, pleading with the Lord that God's people might be true witnesses. He also prayed for the leaders of the government and for the leaders of the Roman Catholic Church. Then he praised God that his real home was in heaven and that his life was hidden in God's hands. Also he was thankful that God's way is perfect, whether it involves going to be with him or staying to work in earth's harvest field. Yona accompanied Ian to the bridge that marks the boundary of Bugesera and then returned to his home. It was a long way to walk.

Darkness fell, and the family heard the sound of soldiers. The six soldiers told the family they had just come to take Yona away for questioning. They drove him back down to the bridge where he had such a short while ago said goodbye to his friend Ian. By the river the soldiers shot Yona and threw his body into the Nyabarongo River.

Sitting nearby and waiting for the same fate was a schoolteacher named Andrew, who knew Yona. He was amazed as he saw Yona walking so calmly, singing hymns as he went to his death. The soldiers also were amazed by his courage and the fact that he prayed for them as they killed him.

It affected them so much that they turned to Andrew and ordered him to go home. He was able to find someone who led him through the bush to the Burundi border and to safety. News of the death of this remarkable man of God and leader of the church spread throughout the world, and his name was added to the list of modern martyrs in the Memorial Chapel in St. Paul's Cathedral, London.

The Coup d'État

In 1965 when elections were held once more, the Parmehutu party maintained control, and Kayibanda returned to power. Once back in office, Kayibanda and his party unleashed a new wave of ethnic hatred, and even the moderate among the Hutu became alarmed. Corruption within the public domain was widespread, violence an everyday occurrence, and measures were taken not just to intimidate Tutsi children at school but also to expel them from every school and university. It was this issue that pushed Habyarimana to stage a coup d'état in 1973. He installed himself as president. The move away from democracy worried the moderate Hutu politicians as well as the few Tutsi who were still in public office, but behind President Habyarimana stood his wife, Agathe, and her very powerful family.

After the coup there was a time of uneasy peace in most of the country, although in Bugesera random murders continued of not only adults but also children. Then there was another outbreak of violence against the Tutsis in Giterama, with the familiar pattern of torching homes, looting, and massacres.

The people were living in constant fear and distrust, even of friends and neighbors. The government had seized the property and land of many of the Rwandese who had fled into exile, and the situation in the country was deteriorating rapidly.

The Emergence of the Rwandan Patriotic Front

In October 1990 the RPF (Rwandan Patriotic Front), an army mainly made of up young men who had been brought up as refugees in Uganda, invaded the northwest of the country at Byumba, hoping to gain control and restore democracy. The Rwandese governmental army was able to quickly repel them and regain control, mainly because they had the help of soldiers from France, Germany, and Congo, even though the RPF was a well-trained and well-disciplined guerrilla force.

The Rwandese government's response to this incursion was swift and bitter. They punished many of the remaining Tutsi, imprisoning thousands of them for so-called collaboration and sentenced them to death. In most cases the death sentence was never carried out, but many still died from malnutrition and torture.

The RPF retreated into Uganda, but during the fighting, their leader, Maj. Gen. Fred Rwigema, had been killed. Paul Kagame took his place, a man who was to feature significantly in Rwanda's future. (Paul Kagame is the current president of Rwanda.)

The fighting around Byumba had caused international concern and a greater awareness of the growing crisis in Rwanda. Pressure was put upon President Habyarimana to come to the negotiating table and engage in talks with the RPF. The Arusha talks were arranged. Although the president agreed to allow the return of refugees under the terms of the Arusha Agreement, he did not ever implement any of the measures agreed on. That is why Kolini and many others like him remained refugees and were forbidden to visit Rwanda. There was a fear of them returning and the balance of power being disturbed.

Habyarimana's signature on the piece of paper seemed enough to satisfy the international community, and they took their eyes off the Rwanda situation, leaving the extremist Hutu party members to intensify their efforts to exterminate the Tutsi population. The radio stations were government controlled and began to pour out vitriolic hate messages to their listeners. This had an enormous effect because many of the people were illiterate, and the radio was their only means of gathering information.

The government drew up a list of Hutu Ten Commandments. They were horrific in their implications, dictating how a Hutu should act toward a Tutsi neighbor or relative. The commandments forbade any personal, social, or business dealings in any form. They imposed severe restrictions on the life of a Tutsi, such as denying access to education, and even forbade taking pity on anyone of Tutsi blood, however great their need appeared. Such things ran completely counter to the Rwandese tradition and culture, yet the Hutu population, for the most part, believed and obeyed these rules. These commandments were printed out and could be found hanging in public places for all to see.

All this propaganda destroyed the self-image of the Tutsi people; some of them began to believe that they were worthless and worthy only of death. Mostly, they tried to lead quiet lives and not stir up any trouble.

In 1992 the Hutu extremists had planned a "dummy run" of genocide in the Bugesera district. If they managed to meet their objectives without incurring the wrath of the international community, then they knew they could implement the master plan of exterminating all Tutsi people. Many people were killed at this time, but some found refuge in churches, schools, and hospitals. These had always been places of refuge in the past when there had been massacres, but tragically in the near future these places would become targets for slaughter and no longer shelters for the innocent.

The Beginning of the Genocide

On April 6, 1994, a rocket attack was launched that brought down the plane in which President Habyarimana was traveling, along with the president of Burundi. They had been in Arusha for further peace negotiations. The plane came down in the president's own backyard, killing everyone on board. It was reported that white-skinned soldiers, believed to be French, were seen running from the only rocket launcher in the country, at Kanombe airport. It is certain that French soldiers had been training Rwandese soldiers and that no African soldier possessed the expertise needed to use such a weapon.

It appeared to initiate a preplanned signal, for within minutes of the radio announcement of the plane crash, well-known Tutsi were rounded up and killed. Death lists had already been prepared and street maps with every house in Kigali marked if it belonged to a Tutsi. There was also a black list of the homes of moderate Hutu who had opposed or even shown concern over the regime's extremist policies.

It took only a few hours for the demonic unleashing of violence to begin. Blame for the launching of the weapon was attributed to the RPF. All the government soldiers and *interahamwe* (as the local bands of killers were called) were already prepared, just waiting for the signal to implement their plan of genocide.

The first victims were the political opponents, and among them was Prime Minister Agathe Uwilingiyimana. She was a moderate Hutu who had worked very hard to try to stand against the extreme policies of the government and bring unity to the country. She was murdered, along with a group of ten Belgian UN peacekeepers assigned to protect her, in her own home by the presidential guard, an elite group of military police under the control of the widow of the president. Her children were miraculously rescued the following day by others of the UN peacekeeping force. It was a nightmare for the UN peacekeeping mission, as they had no brief allowing them to counter the violence they saw erupting around them, and they were forced to witness mass murder of civilians while being unable to help.

When violence broke out with such ferocity, the RPF again invaded from Uganda and began to march on Kigali with a force of four thousand troops. The intent was to stop the bloodshed and restore democracy. They were skilled fighters, many of whom were fighting for their families and friends, hoping to save them from the genocide.

The radio was about the only means the population had of knowing what was happening, and messages were being broadcast instructing listeners to stay calm and remain in their homes. However, in certain areas they were told to gather in churches or schools for their safety. This was a ploy of the government and caused its victims to become "sitting ducks" waiting for their attackers. When people did try to flee to the bush or to get to the borders for safety, they frequently met roadblocks of *interahamwe* waiting for them with guns and machetes.

All over the country the gangs of *interahamwe* roamed the hills and valleys, killing randomly every person they perceived might be a Tutsi or who opposed the present regime. All schools and churches were closed, and even soccer matches and community activities were stopped so that everyone could be forced into taking part in the "work" of ethnic cleansing. Machetes were the weapons most often used because China had shipped supplies of them into the country and almost everyone was skilled in using this tool in everyday life. Axes, hoes, clubs with studded nails, as well as firearms, were also used. There was a policy to torture and degrade the *inyenzi* (cockroaches), as the Tutsi were called, before killing them. Often men and women faced the agony of seeing their children dismembered before their very eyes as they awaited their own, often slow, death. Women were often stripped and gang-raped in public, right on the road. Sometimes this continued until death mercifully released them, though many of the women were spared to live with HIV infection and the shame of their defilement. Pregnant mothers had their babies cut out of their wombs and then were left to bleed to death. Other women were raped purely with the intent of infecting them with HIV/AIDS to give them a slow death. No one was shown mercy.

Kolini, commenting on the horrors of the genocide, especially the rape of women, said that rape was not committed to satisfy a lustful, sexual desire. That would have been terrible enough, but it was done purely to degrade and destroy the women. It was done publicly, often in the middle of a road. The rapists never stopped to think, "This could be my sister or my aunt, my mother or grandmother." It was just someone to hurt and degrade.

The womb in Rwandese culture was a sacred place that expressed love and the source of life. A woman was honored because she is the source of life. Indeed, before the genocide a woman was not ever regarded as belonging to a particular ethnic grouping; she was above that as a life carrier.

Children were also to be protected because of their innocence. An enemy could be killed in self-defense, but never an innocent child. An elderly person was the "library of today," the source of wisdom. When people needed advice, they visited an old person who had experience of life to guide them. Neither a woman, nor a child, nor an older person should ever be destroyed. These traditional values vanished in the genocide.

The horror of those days is unimaginable as Rwanda underwent the fastest genocide known in modern times. It is estimated that over a million people were slaughtered in just one hundred days. Mass graves are still being discovered, so the true number may never be known.

Many terrified Tutsi sought refuge in the only place they thought they might be safe, the church. Thousands were packed into tiny mud-brick churches through the length and breadth of Rwanda, and here, thousands met their death. In some of these churches the people were betrayed by their own pastors into the hands of the killers. In other places the pastors were murdered as they tried to defend their people.

When the RPF finally liberated the country, the violence may have been over, but the terror was still living in the hearts of the people. Traumatic shock, guilt, fear, and profound loss were emotions that all the survivors had to live with, no matter which side they had been on. The church in all denominations was left in disarray, riddled with guilt because of complicity, and bereft of leaders who had been massacred, had fled, or were imprisoned.

God put his broken church on the hearts of men and women like Kolini and Freda, causing them to pray that someone would go and help. God provided this help by calling them to come and take over the reins of his church in Rwanda. The Lord would rebuild his church in Rwanda under new leadership, because according to Matthew 16:18, not even the gates of hades would be able to overcome it.

CHAPTER 12

The Call
Back to Rwanda

T hroughout the years when Kolini was living and working
in Congo, he took a very real interest in what was happening in
Rwanda. From time to time he had opportunity to visit until
the political situation became so volatile that it was impossible
to do so. There were times when the Congolese rebels were fighting in Rwanda, and because he had a Congolese passport, he
was restricted from entering the country. Nevertheless, Rwanda
was still on his heart and in his prayers, especially the Anglican
Church as reports reached him during 1994–1995 that all the
bishops had run away into exile. Kolini's constant prayer was
that there would be those who would help the struggling church
and the survivors of genocide.

In 1994 Kolini was given a six-month sabbatical leave by the Congolese church to study at St. John's College at the University of Durham in England. On his way back home at the completion of his time there, he had arranged a visit in Kenya. There he met George Carey, the archbishop of Canterbury, who was preparing to visit Rwanda. There was a need for someone to accompany the archbishop who knew the country, could speak its language, and understood the political scene. Kolini was pleased to undertake this duty. His friend from Uganda, John Rucyahana, went with them for the two-week visit. During that time Kolini and John were able to make an assessment of the state of the Anglican Church. They traveled around all the dioceses and collected information to write a report. They also, under the auspices of AEE, were able to organize a pastors' conference to encourage the priests who had suffered so much and who were still ministering faithfully.

All the bishops had fled Rwanda and were trying to hold court from Kenya. Kolini and John spoke openly against these bishops, who seemed to be operating on the Catholic premise that the church is where the bishops are, rather than vice versa. The only bishop who faithfully returned from time to time to visit his diocese was Bishop Onesiphore of Byumba.

Tensions were very high, and there was a power struggle between opposing groups within the St. Etienne Cathedral in Kigali. Some of the members supported the newly self-appointed bishop of Kigali and faced one direction to worship; while many of the returnees protested his position, supported the former archbishop, and turned their backs on the altar to worship facing the opposite direction. The diocese of Kigali had decided to create a "crisis committee" to run the church, writing to the archbishop of Canterbury about the situation. This letter provoked a meeting of the Anglican Consultative Council in Panama, and it took the unusual step of telling the bishops in exile that they must return within three months to their dioceses or lose their positions as bishops within the church.

The report that Kolini and John wrote after their visit was presented not only to the church authorities but also to the new Rwandese government. The bishops in exile were upset when they saw this report, and it caused friction between them and Kolini, which was a problem he had to face when he eventually became the primate of Rwanda.

The following year there was another opportunity for Kolini to visit Rwanda and encourage the pastors there. He was still burdened in prayer for someone to go and help the church, which had been hugely damaged during the genocide. He was completely unaware that he might become the answer to his own prayers.

Meanwhile the church in Congo was also going through a difficult time, and these problems escalated in 1997. Kolini was overdue for a sabbatical leave and had been accepted to attend the Virginia Theological Seminary in the United States. This removed him from a very volatile situation not only in the Anglican Church but also in the country that was on the verge of another civil war.

This time Freda was not able to go with her husband when he went away for study and rest. The family needed her, as there were eight children to care for: Christopher, John, Heri (Harry), Amani, Joanna, David, Joy, and Anna. Freda had never lost the love for her own country of Rwanda, and all through the troubles she had constantly prayed for her people. Through the time of genocide, she really didn't think that the Rwandan Patriotic Front (formed in 1987 by the Tutsi refugee diaspora in Uganda) would be victorious. When they were victorious, she heard with delight about the many refugees who were returning to their homeland after years of exile.

It reminded her of the Scriptures that spoke of the children of Israel returning to their homeland from all the corners of the world. Even some of the Rwandese who lived around them in Congo began to return, and in her heart was also a growing longing to go home again. As she prayed, she asked the Lord, "Am I to stay in Shaba by myself?" She talked to the Lord constantly, telling him that she was happy to serve him in Congo but that one day she wanted to return to her own land. She believed that the Lord would make this happen. Freda was very aware that although her husband had a burden for Rwanda, he had no thoughts of returning.

About this time someone challenged Kolini, saying, "Why don't you go to Rwanda and shepherd those people? They have no shepherd." Kolini replied, "I have no reason to go. I have my own diocese. I'm not ready to leave my province to go to another, and my diocese still needs me; so forget it!"

Freda had accompanied Kolini to Australia and New Zealand just before he flew to the seminary in Virginia. As she returned to Congo, people asked her, "Why are you arriving at a time when we are leaving because of the war in Congo?" Freda's answer was, "This is my home!" Many people were evacuating because there was a fresh outbreak of civil war and the rebel army was fighting in Goma. The rebels were intending to advance through the country and take Kinshasa. Hundreds of people were being killed, and as always, Rwandese nationals were targets for violent attacks.

About four days after Freda's return from Australia and New Zealand to Lubumbashi, a soldier appeared at the gate of the church compound. He asked to speak urgently to the bishop. When it was explained to him that Kolini was not in the country, he then asked to speak to Freda, but in private.

The watchman from the gate came to ask Freda if she would see this man, but she was feeling very tired and asked that the soldier give his message to her staff at the gate. Freda thought it was just another Congolese person who had come to ask for help, so she told the watchman to take care of the man.

The soldier would not give his message to any of Freda's staff, he declined money, and he would not go away. He sat quietly and patiently on a bench in the office for two hours. Eventually, someone came into the office who asked him again what he needed. Once again, the soldier stated that he had come with a message for the bishop. Since the bishop was away, the soldier needed to deliver it to the bishop's wife, but she had refused to see him. Then the questioner asked if the soldier would trust him with the message, and he agreed. They went into a room where they could be undisturbed.

"Look, you can see that I am a soldier," the visitor explained. "I am intelligent and, for my part, I want nothing from this lady.

My heart told me that I must come and warn her that tonight this house will be attacked. Their names are on the rebels' list, and it is marked for 1900 hours. Tell them to make sure that all the children are safely at home and to lock the doors. These soldiers are not local men who know these are good people; they have come from far away. I have come because if a person knows that something like this is going to happen but does not do anything about it, then the blood is on their hands. That is why I have come." The soldier was alluding to Ezekiel 33:3–6.

The soldier left and the member of staff went to Freda with the message. Freda was suspicious, but the fact that this soldier did not ask for anything and that he even refused some money for transportation made her think the warning was genuine. She thought maybe he would return the next day and demand money, but the person giving her the message reminded her that it was eleven o'clock in the morning and that the deadline given to them for the attack was for seven that night. As they talked about the message, they felt that it was a genuine warning and that they should act on it. It was very hard to be sure or to know how to react, as the *interahamwe* in the Rwandese genocide had so often counseled people to stay with all their family behind locked doors. When they then attacked, all the family were like sitting ducks just waiting for their abusers.

Freda called her older boys and told them about the warning, but they were disinclined to believe the story. It was then that Freda thought of a way in which she might find out the truth. She would send her messenger—who was totally trustworthy and a Hutu—to talk to a Hutu who was in a position of authority and who was also known to be antagonistic to the Kolini family. Freda quickly arranged for a car to take her messenger to see this man. He was to be dropped off about half a mile away, so that no one would know he had come from the bishop's house.

This all went according to plan. When her messenger first challenged the Hutu leader about what he had heard, it was vehemently denied. The leader was defensive, denying everything and demanding to know where this information had come from. The messenger stayed calm and admitted he did not know the person who had spread this rumor. The leader then went to confer with others and eventually returned with the information that, indeed, there was a plan to exterminate the family that night.

The precious hours were ticking away like a time bomb, but in due course Freda's messenger arrived back safely at the compound without being suspected of being a spy. Having received this confirmation, Freda then went to see two of their close friends, one a Pentecostal missionary and the other, a Brethren. She told them the story and asked for their advice as to what she should do. The Pentecostal friend felt she should do as the soldier had told her, to gather all the family together and lock the doors. Freda was not very reassured by his advice, since one bullet or grenade would break the lock on the door and they would be left defenseless. She had secretly hoped her friend might offer to come with his car and take them all to his house.

Then Freda went to her Brethren friends who were *muzungu* missionaries. They did not offer to hide the family either, but they did go to the government officials and inform them that they had every reason to believe that the bishop's house was going to be attacked that night.

The officials kept questioning the source of the information, and the missionaries told them that Mrs. Kolini had been told and that it had since been verified. The fact that white people had come to the government officials meant that they had to do something about it, or there could be an international outcry if the truth was given to the international press. They sent some government soldiers to guard the house, but only for the hours of darkness. They didn't want it to become known that they were protecting these people, and their own soldiers did not want to be seen or recognized. However, they did guard the house until the day the family left.

Freda's Dilemma

Freda considered her options of leaving Congo or staying. As she prayed about her decision, Freda felt that she could not abandon the diocese, especially while her husband was in Virginia. It seemed as if she would be leaving a sinking ship, and she could not do that despite all the pleading from the people around her. She did feel, however, that she should try to get exit visas for all the children and have their papers in order and ready for an evacuation, should that prove necessary. However, the threats to their well-being became increasingly real and the situation ever more acute.

Freda was not able just to flee to Zambia with her children because within the compound there were about thirty people. She could not take them all nor leave some behind. If she took them all to Zambia, how would she find shelter or money for food? How she was missing the help and support of Kolini, who was so far away in Virginia!

Sonja Hoekstra-Foss, an Anglican missionary from the United States, had been a good friend of the family since her arrival in Congo in 1987. Sonja and Freda talked through the idea of Freda going to Rwanda to find a way to get the younger children there. The older children were already in boarding schools in Rwanda. Sonja would remain and look after the younger ones until Freda returned. Having agreed on this plan, Sonja managed to get the airplane ticket that Freda needed, and she flew to Rwanda via Zambia. While she was in Zambia, Freda and Kolini talked by telephone, and she told him what she was doing. He posed a question that troubled her: "If they close the borders, what will you do?" It was like a prophecy and lay heavily on her. From Zambia Freda flew to Entebbe, Uganda, and stayed a night in Kampala before continuing the journey to Kigali, Rwanda.

On the Sunday morning after her arrival, Freda went to St. Etienne Cathedral to worship. On Tuesday she received an alarming message from her husband. He had received a telephone call from missionaries in Congo to say that their house had been attacked by rebels looking for Kolini and Freda.

Before Freda had left Congo, she had entrusted Sonja with the exit visas and papers for the children, and Sonja had promised to try to get them out of the country and to a place of safety if they were in danger. For two days the soldiers came to the house, and the children hid wherever they could. On the third day the soldiers attacked the house. The children were all at school, so Sonja rushed to get them from school to the airport to put them on a plane to Zambia. All seemed to be going well until one airport official refused to stamp the children's documents. He tried to arrest and imprison the children, but another official at the airport, who knew Kolini, objected to his actions, protesting loudly that it was a breach of the law to imprison children. He said they had to let the children go, even if the rebels searched for the parents. The authorities did allow the children to leave the building with Sonja, but they kept all the documents.

Sonja took the children back to her house. She found someone who would take passport photos of the children and then quickly went to the immigration department and procured, by God's intervention, a fresh set of documents. After two weeks Sonja was able to take the children overland out of the country into Zambia. This amazing woman had kept her promise to Freda, and the children were safe. When relating this story to me, Freda exclaimed, "May God bless Sonja without measure for all she did for the Kolini family!"

Meanwhile, a very anxious mother was making plans to return to Zambia, not knowing the children were free, thinking that she would be physically nearer to them and maybe they would sense that she was close by. She knew that if she returned to Congo, it would mean certain death for her and all the children, if they were with her.

With these plans all laid, Freda was sitting in a house in Kigali with a group of women. These women did not know her or her story. She was very quiet and preoccupied with her own troubles when they began to talk in Kinyarwanda and tell the story of a mother who had put some of her children in school in Rwanda, leaving the others in Congo while her husband was in the United States and that following her arrival the borders were closed. The women wondered how this family could be reunited. As they discussed this question, Freda kept quiet. The following day when she had news that her children were safe in Zambia, she told these women that she was the mother about whom they had been talking. Then her tears could flow, and they praised God together.

The next day Freda was able to go to Uganda, and at Entebbe Airport she found Kolini's friend from college so many years before, Bishop Geoffrey, waiting for her. The children were flown from Zambia to meet her there. All the extended family and friends from the compound in Lubumbashi had escaped and were with them. Bishop Geoffrey arranged transportation from the airport to the Namirembe guesthouse at the cathedral in Kampala and then more transportation for traveling through Uganda and into Rwanda. This was no small undertaking for such a large group of people. Eventually, they all arrived safely and the family was reunited. Freda's prayers had been answered, as the Lord had brought her back to Rwanda, but not quite in the way she had envisioned.

Throughout this crisis, Kolini had been telephoning daily to Congo, Rwanda, and Zambia, trying to find out what was happening to his beloved family. When Freda was safely in Rwanda with all her children, she began to look for a permanent home for them all; but Kolini was very unsure about this. His heart was still with his flock in Congo. He was still bishop of Shaba, and as far as he could see, the Lord wanted him to return there. He had received no direct guidance to tell him otherwise. His own parents and Freda's parents also had fled Congo and were back in Rwanda. He was married to Freda, but he was also married to the church. What was he to do? He was in constant prayer about his situation.

There was disquiet within the Anglican Church in Rwanda. The bishops who had fled to Kenya had been given an ultimatum, to either return to their dioceses within three months or lose their offices as bishops. Only one bishop had a true shepherd's heart; Onesiphore from Byumba chose to return and care for his flock. Even the bishop of Kigali chose not to return. The synod then decided to write to Kolini, asking if he would be willing to come to the province and serve as bishop of Kigali. At this time he was still studying in Virginia.

As Kolini prayed, he felt that perhaps it was not just a coincidence that his wife and family were already living in Kigali and that for years he had been praying for someone to be willing to go and help the church there in all its difficulties. He heard the Lord speak to him as he prayed, "You are praying for someone to help Rwanda; it is you!"

Once he had heard the voice of the Lord speaking to him, Kolini's mind was made up. He could see the way forward. He first went to Kigali for a brief visit to see his family, and then he returned to Congo to call an extraordinary synod. At this meeting he handed in his resignation, so that the process could begin to elect his successor. Next he went to the house of bishops in Bunia to ask them to release him and give him a recommendation as a bishop to serve the Anglican Church of Rwanda. Rwanda had become a separate Anglican province in 1992, as had Burundi and Congo.

These formalities completed, Kolini was then free to return to Rwanda and was duly enthroned as the bishop of Kigali in St. Etienne Cathedral in August 1997.

CHAPTER 13

Background History of the Anglican Church of Rwanda

W hat kind of church did Kolini come to help when he left Congo and agreed to be bishop of Kigali and later archbishop in Rwanda? It is helpful to understand how the Anglican Church of Rwanda was founded and the legacy that Kolini inherited, so that it can be appreciated how much he has been able to achieve in the ten years he has been in the leadership role.

After the First World War, the League of Nations divided up the territories previously ruled by Germany, and so Ruanda-Urundi was allocated to Belgium in 1919. This decision was later ratified in 1923. The country had to get used to another colonial power, which spoke French rather than the Flemish the German rulers had used. Some of the borders of the country were also changed, which was very confusing for the population that was largely illiterate. The new borders of 1910 took no notice of ethnic groupings, and that is why there are about three million Kinyarwanda-speaking Rwandese still living in both Congo and western Uganda.

In 1914, as part of their military service during the First World War, two young Christian doctors went to Mengo Hospital in Kampala, Uganda. While they were there, both were challenged concerning the spiritual needs of the people in Ruanda-Urundi. Dr. Arthur Stanley Smith and Dr. Leonard Sharpe set out on a safari into eastern Rwanda and began teaching and preaching at a village called Gahini on the shores of Lake Muhazi. In those days such a safari was extremely dangerous and difficult, with no real roads to travel on, just mud tracks and always the possibility of encountering wild animals. Ugandans had to be recruited to be porters to carry all their equipment and baggage, mostly on their heads. It was a risky adventure for them, but they felt sure the Lord was telling them to take the gospel into Rwanda and Burundi, as these countries are now called. These two doctors were both Anglicans, so this was the very first introduction of the Anglican Church to Rwanda.

The two doctors both returned as missionaries to western Uganda after the war, founding a hospital at Kabale very near to the border with Rwanda. During their years working at Kabale, they were always burdened for Rwanda and Burundi and believed God had promised them an entry to evangelize in these countries. Several times they applied for permission to start a medical work in Rwanda, and eventually this was granted.

In the days before the Council of Vatican II, the relationship between the Roman Catholic Church and the Protestant churches was difficult and strained. There was very little dialogue between the two groups, and a great deal of suspicion and jealousy existed. Such attitudes made it very difficult for these pioneer missionaries to establish their work in Rwanda. The state-backed Catholic Church had a strong influence over the chiefs, so much so that they were threatened with being deposed from their positions and their lands confiscated if they dared to cooperate with the Protestant missionaries.

However, despite these setbacks, the two doctors persevered with their work, showing God's love through medical ministry as well as preaching. They realized that even with the difficulties they faced, they still had an open door to take the gospel into Rwanda. They encouraged others to join them when they wrote home. The CMS also saw the potential of this new venture and gave its blessing, so the Ruanda Mission[1] was formed. The first baptism of new converts took place at Gahini in 1926. They were baptized by Rev. Harold Guillebaud, who had joined the mission team with his wife, Margaret. He was a gifted linguist who translated the Bible into Kinyarwandan and also gave the church its first hymnbook, which is, although revised, still in use today. The children, grandchildren, and great-grandchildren of this couple are still giving service to the Lord as missionaries in Rwanda and Burundi.

From these small beginnings the Anglican Church in Rwanda has grown to approximately one million adherents in 2007, and that in a country whose entire population is around nine million. God has indeed blessed and increased the work that began in such a small way and with many difficulties. It has taken many years for the deep divisions between the Roman Catholic Church and Protestant churches to be healed.

The early missionaries, like the Catholics, also focused much of their evangelism on the Tutsi people because they were in most of the positions of authority and leadership in the country. It was believed that if they could be converted to Christ, then they would use their influence to win others. In that way the whole country could be evangelized more efficiently. The missionaries worked very hard to produce a Kinyarwanda-English grammar, as well as a Bible and hymnbook. Literacy classes were held to teach people to read the Bible for themselves. Probably because of the very close association with the high-born Tutsi people, the language used was a very pure form of Kinyarwanda, such as was spoken in the royal court. All these factors made it appear as if they favored the Tutsi people over the Hutu and laid a foundation, albeit unknowingly, that would cause problems in later years when the racial conflict emerged.

The Church Advances

One of the big advances for the Anglican Church was the establishment of a secondary school at Shyogwe. Since the early beginnings of the mission at Gahini, the CMS had given the name Ruanda General and Medical Mission to the developing work in Rwanda. From the original mission station that was built in 1922 at Gahini, the outreach had spread northward and westward to two new places, Shyira and Kigeme. Mission stations were established in both of these places, and eventually they became the seats of dioceses.

The Holy Spirit began to work in very powerful ways, and revival occurred in these places. The believers did not want to keep the wonderful blessings they were experiencing to themselves, so they began to go in small groups traveling throughout the country and sharing their testimonies. Many people believed the message of salvation through faith in Jesus and joined the church.

Until this time there had been only a couple of primary schools established by the mission, which taught the basics of reading and writing to help new believers read for themselves. Then it became apparent that there was a need for a secondary school. All of the children who completed primary school and wished to continue with their education had to compete for admissioin in the Catholic secondary school. So the mission applied to the colonial government for a plot of land, and in 1944 it was granted a place called Shyogwe, on the top of a hill and in the center of the country. It took time to build the school because it was just after the Second World War and building materials were in very short supply. On June 28, 1946, the school officially opened with seventy-five pupils attending—all boys, working and living in the partially completed complex. The school continued to be built and to expand over the next five years and was highly regarded by the postwar Belgian government.[2]

Revival

When I talk to people in Great Britain and they learn that I have visited Rwanda frequently, I find their immediate reaction is to associate the country with one of three things: gorillas, genocide, or revival.

The Rwandese church, springing from the early days of the Episcopal Church and the Ruanda Mission, did experience times of blessing and revival. I was there for some of this blessing when I lived and worked in Uganda in the 1960s. I am often asked and, like many others, have pondered this question myself: How could a church that has been so singularly blessed later become involved in genocide? Emmanuel Kolini and Peter Holmes have sought to answer this question in their recent book, *Christ Walks Where Evil Reigned: Responding to the Rwandan Genocide.*[3]

Revival, as defined in the *Concise Oxford Dictionary*, is "the bringing back of a religious fervor." Although the Christian gospel had been faithfully taught in Rwanda, over the decades something of the impact of the transforming life of Jesus in the individual had been lost, and it was a renewal of this that the Holy Spirit brought at this time. The revival movement began in 1935–1936 in Kabale in Uganda and Gahini in Rwanda, and it continued in waves until the 1960s. By then it had spread throughout most of the Great Lakes region of Central and East Africa.

The teachings of the revival emphasized personal holiness springing from an intimate relationship with God. Such a relationship then spread to an openness and honesty among believers. Openness of spirit is not the norm in the traditional

Rwandese culture in which people prefer to keep their secrets to themselves. It could only be a work of God through his Spirit that would break down such barriers between people, allowing them to begin to trust each other, no matter from which ethnic group they originated.

The Scriptures that the Holy Spirit emphasized during the revival were taken from 1 John 1:5–10 and speak of walking in the light, and this became the main characteristic of the movement.

> This is the message we have heard from him and declare to you: God is light; in him there is no darkness at all. If we claim to have fellowship with him yet walk in the darkness, we lie and do not live by the truth. But if we walk in the light, as he is in the light, we have fellowship with one another, and the blood of Jesus, his Son, purifies us from all sin.
>
> If we claim to be without sin, we deceive ourselves and the truth is not in us. If we confess our sins, he is faithful and just and will forgive us our sins and purify us from all unrighteousness. If we claim we have not sinned, we make him out to be a liar and his word has no place in our lives.

In his book *A History of Global Anglicanism*, Kevin Ward stated, "The East African Revival . . . has had a profound impact on the character of East African Anglicanism as a whole, and indeed far beyond the Anglican Church."[4] This impact was seen and felt as the Holy Spirit convicted believers, and they openly confessed their anger and hatred against each other. Hutu and Tutsi Christians began to accept each other as brothers and sisters, one flesh in the Lord. It helped missionaries and Africans alike to see that in God's eyes they were all equal when they stood at the foot of the cross. No one was superior and no one was inferior. There was a wonderful bonding as missionaries and their African brothers and sisters wept together in repentance, and together they found the forgiveness of God and began to walk together as equals in the Lord. There was a great emphasis on a daily cleansing from all known sin and walking in the light.

It resulted in a new attitude of living in openness with each other and the Lord. This was the result of renewed intimacy with Jesus, and it also had a horizontal effect of uniting believers in a new closeness. Personal disciplines of prayer and Bible study were also encouraged, as well as the believers meeting together each week for times of confession, prayer, and Bible teaching.

In a traditionally male-dominated society, where a wife was often regarded as a possession of the husband rather than as an equal within the marriage, the revival movement also brought changes within the homes, reflecting Jesus' attitude toward women, treating them as equals within the kingdom of God.

In her book *Rwanda: The Land God Forgot?* Meg Guillebaud wrote about the Tutsi women of those days: "Many high born Tutsi [women] were not allowed to be seen outside their *rugo* [the enclosure around their houses]. When they insisted in joining fellowship meetings and going to church, it was misunderstood and led to much persecution. . . . During the Revival days it was impossible to muzzle the women. Once they had experienced acceptance in Christ, they wanted to tell everyone what He meant to them. They joined teams going to other villages to tell of what God had done for them."[5]

The attitude of some of the men changed toward women, and they honored them because the Lord was pouring his Spirit on them equally. Not only were the racial and ethnic values challenged, but also the gender issues. It was, however, only at a very local and individual level that these changes took place; they did not affect the wider society. It was a fact that even in the church many women were dishonored in the genocide, as if the revival lessons had never been learned.

When the revival took place, not everyone, even within the Rwanda Mission, was sure that this was a real work of God. Some of the missionaries were skeptical and others openly antagonistic toward what they saw happening in the Anglican churches, schools, and mission compounds. These people kept themselves apart from the movement to the extent that it almost caused a schism within both the church and the mission. Some of the manifestations that occurred when believers were filled by the Holy Spirit were very disturbing to some people, and as always when God is at work, the Enemy did some counterfeiting. This lack of solidarity among the mission family weakened the revival movement, and it has been suggested that this is one reason why there was no lasting impact that might have helped prevent the genocide.

Tharcisse Gatwa, in his book *The Churches and Ethnic Ideology in the Rwanda Crises 1900–1994*, noted: "The 1930s Protestant revival . . . was rather timid and its ground so narrowed by its spiritual leaders to personal and family conversion that it did little to challenge structural injustices." He added, "The new converts wanted the missionaries to attack the feudal, social and political injustices as well as colonialism. . . .The C.M.S. missionaries wanted evil to be treated only in a private, individual, familial context."[6]

The revival movement brought a wonderful new life and enthusiasm to individual believers, restoring their relationship with both the Lord and their fellow Christians, but it did not reach out to address the wider social issues that faced the whole country, including the emerging racism. And although many people in Rwanda embraced Christianity as the gospel was preached, it was not always also understood that the traditional ancestral gods needed to be rejected. So a situation evolved where some of the new Christians still held on to old beliefs, which led to confusion and created a foothold for the Enemy within the growing and revived church. Conversely, the church tried to change some of the existing Rwandese culture, ignoring many good traditions and imposing a Western-style structure in an African situation. This also weakened the emerging church. So when the fires of hatred between the Tutsi and Hutu peoples were kindled, the church was powerless to extinguish the flames and even, unwittingly, took part in fanning them.

Church Politics

As the Anglican Church grew in Rwanda, and with the many new converts who were saved through the revival, churches were built, and a need arose for trained indigenous pastors. There was no Anglican theological college in Rwanda, so candidates for ordination were mostly sent to Bishop Tucker College at Mukono, Uganda. In 1965 there was great joy when twelve Rwandese men were ordained as deacons at Gahini.[7]

With more trained priests available, the first diocese was established in Rwanda in 1965. The diocese covered the whole of the country. Rev. Adonia Sebununguri was elected as bishop, but his appointment was not without jealousy and controversy. It was the beginning of a period of strife among the leadership of the church that caused much bitterness and heartache for many believers. Nevertheless, by 1966 the leadership of the Anglican Church was handed over completely to Rwandans, and the missionary bishops withdrew.

During this time another wave of ethnic unrest occurred, and many Tutsi people were marginalized and abused. The church failed to stand against the increasing violence, even though it was a spiritually growing church. By 1970 the Anglican Church was the largest Protestant denomination. A second diocese was formed in the early 1970s at the university city of Butare. It served the southern half of the country, and the bishop elected to serve it was Bishop Ndandari.

Quarrels began between the two bishops from the time that Bishop Ndandari was enthroned, and the situation worsened in

1975 when it was decided that a third diocese should be formed at Shyira, in the northern part of Rwanda. Both bishops put forward a candidate whom they wanted to become the new bishop of Shyira. The province at that time—from 1970 onward—was the Francophone area of Burundi, Congo (then still called Zaire), Rwanda, and Uganda. The matter was further complicated because the archbishop for the province was from Uganda. This meant quarrels then spread throughout the whole province, with spiritual and political repercussions. When the candidate whom Bishop Sebununguri had put forward was elected to be the new bishop of Shyira, Bishop Ndandari was very bitter and resentful. When he was due for reelection as archbishop and failed to win the vote, his resentment grew even more intense.

His eventual successor as archbishop was the Reverend Samuel Sindamuka, who was a friend of both Bishop Sebununguri of Kigali and Bishop Nshamihiga of Shyira. These three men had been in league together to depose Bishop Ndandari as archbishop when he had refused to resign of his own accord. The quarrels had become so bitter and so public that the government of Rwanda had intervened, and the minister of justice signed a decree that forced the archbishop out of office and installed Rev. Sindamuka in his place.[8]

The deposed archbishop was still bishop of Butare, and his priests were scandalized at what had happened. They protested outside the Ministry of Justice in Kigali on May 13–19, 1991. Forty-nine priests took part, wearing their robes and carrying placards and Bibles. Other Protestant leaders became involved and tried to act as mediators, pleading with the three bishops to be reconciled, but their efforts were in vain.

The situation was further complicated in 1992 because there were already moves afoot to make Rwanda a separate province and, likewise, Congo and Burundi. In an effort to thwart this, the aggrieved bishop of Butare, the Reverend Ndandari, split his diocese without consultation and ordained three bishops to serve at the new sees of Shyogwe, Kigeme, and Cyangugu and another assistant bishop to serve with him at Butare. He supposed that these four new bishops would side with him in the house of bishops and give him greater power in any forthcoming votes. However, although these men had been ordained by Bishop Ndandari, they were not recognized by the province because they had not been elected according to the canon law.

Eventually, the worldwide Anglican Communion began a mediation process, and the situation was finally settled in 1992 with Rwanda becoming a province in its own right with Bishop Nshamihigo from Shyira as the new archbishop. The bishops who had been ordained to serve in the new dioceses, which Bishop Ndandari had formed in the west of the country, were reconsecrated in the approved way. Another new diocese was also formed in the southeast at Kibungo. These measures calmed the situation to some extent, although antipathy remained beneath the surface. In the following couple of years, as the political situation became increasingly tense and the ethnic divide worsened, the problems began to reemerge when elections began for some more bishops.

During 1993 and into 1994, until the genocide disrupted the whole country, the leaders of the Anglican Church continued to fight with each other, abusing their power and not caring as shepherds ought to care for the flocks for which they are responsible. These leaders rendered themselves morally powerless to give the spiritual help and guidance so desperately needed in 1994 when genocide erupted.

Even the opportunities that the church did have each week to broadcast on the radio and to communicate to the people of Rwanda were not used very effectively, and the church lost credibility at this time. Out in the parishes there were many faithful pastors who were leading their people well, but the senior leadership had failed them at a time when it was most needed. Indeed, as history now sadly illustrates, some of the bishops and other senior clergy became involved in genocide. Even those who did not become actively involved often failed to speak out publicly and protest against events.

How tragic it is that 1994, which had been declared a year of peace in Rwanda by various Christian groups and was welcomed in by an all-night prayer meeting on New Year's Eve, would be the year of the bloodbath of genocide. It was as if people, including many Christians, shut the doors of their consciences and allowed the demonic realm to enter. The lessons of the revival had been forgotten.

CHAPTER 14

Archbishop of Rwanda

In September 1997, only a month after Kolini had been enthroned as the bishop of Kigali, elections began to find an archbishop for the province. After all the problems and trauma of the previous years, the church needed a strong leader. Kolini had been nominated, but although he was the most senior bishop, not everyone was sure that he was the person to hold the position. There were some people who felt that he was a foreigner and may not understand the situation. This church did not have a good track record; it was a shattered church carrying its own deep shame. Also, there were still warring factions within the church leadership. On a human level it would be an almost impossible task to bring these factions together and unite the clergy to preach the gospel and disciple the people once again.

Kolini was asked many questions, and he remembers one in particular: "What is your vision for the church?" His response was, "I am not sure, but I know that I have to understand the church and listen to the Lord and ask him what we should do."

This honest answer must have impressed the inquirers because Kolini was elected and enthroned as the new archbishop of Rwanda. It would prove to be a huge challenge to help the church move forward in the aftermath of the genocide.

Kolini knew that the church could not move ahead as it was; it must not remain the same church carrying on with the same routines. There had to be major changes. He could not adopt a "wait and see" policy; he had to take decisive actions, sooner rather than later. It is never easy for a leader to come in and make sweeping changes, but things had gone so severely wrong that this was the only way forward. Kolini saw Rwanda as the classroom where the Lord had placed him to learn new lessons.

One question he thought about was, What went wrong with evangelism in Rwanda? As he meditated on this, he was reminded of the parable Jesus told concerning the sower and the seed. The ground needed to be tilled and prepared. That was the challenge. How do you prepare the soil for a plentiful harvest? The soil itself does not change, but it does matter how it is prepared.

How could he help the church to present the gospel in a new way? Past methods had obviously failed; otherwise, how could the church have condoned and even have taken part in the genocide? What had occurred in Rwanda was a challenge to the gospel. There had been one hundred years of missionary and church activity, one hundred years of being "Christianized and civilized," but so-called civilized, educated men with university degrees were those who had planned and practiced genocide. There needed to be a new definition of education, because as Kolini began to see it, education should be uplifting and enable a person to become more fully human, rather than be led by brutal instinct, as happened in 1994.

Did the colonial era make people like robots, programmed to do certain jobs rather like taming an animal to do work? Is this what had happened to the Rwandese? Kolini wanted to understand why the gospel, even after revival, had not really changed hearts and annulled racial divisions.

How could he, as the archbishop, understand killings that happened within a family? Uncles killed nephews; children slaughtered parents; parents slaughtered children. What had Rwanda gained from Western civilization? Humanly speaking, nothing. Yes, the population had books. They were able to read and write, but had it made them better people? Had becoming literate changed their hearts?

These questions confronted Kolini as he thought about the new role he was to fulfill. Unless the gospel made a profound difference in the human heart and changed people, then there was no answer. At best, the church had remained silent during the genocide and, at worst, actively participated. The church and its leadership had failed to be the prophetic voice that it should have been.

It was easy to look back and blame the system, but what was the force behind the system? For Kolini, it was the enemy Satan, who was getting his revenge. He was angry at the gospel being preached throughout the country and the resulting revival that began in Rwanda and then spread in a powerful way throughout East Africa. The Devil was demonstrating his power. Whereas the gospel of Jesus brings life, Satan is the murderous thief out to steal, kill, and destroy.

With the legacy of colonialization, liberalism infiltrated the church, and the Enemy went to work. When the social revolution took place in Rwanda in 1959, the church failed to see that this was an evil that could destroy it. However, the Enemy can only do his work when he has the cooperation of people willing to obey him. His power is broken when people refuse to do evil.

Kolini pondered and prayed a great deal over the state of the church and how he could lead it forward. He was sure that when the Lord sent the revival, it was no mistake, no accident. He was convinced that the church needed to go back to the gospel that was preached during the revival in order to bring healing and reconciliation back to the church. Of course, politics also has a major part to play in rebuilding a nation, but politics does not deal with the human heart.

Kolini quoted to me two texts paraphrased from the Kinyarwanda Bible: "A righteous people are a blessing to any nation" (Proverbs 14:34) and "Where there is no righteousness the people perish" (Proverbs 29:18). He went on to explain that in his view politics can be a servant of the gospel, but it should never be the other way around—the gospel as the servant of politics. People are changed by the gospel of

Jesus, and people living in his righteousness are a blessing to the nation.

So, in taking up his new post as archbishop, Kolini faced huge challenges. How was he to deal with the situation he found in the church? How do you turn a sick, confused, and broken society full of widows, orphans, and prisoners and their families into a reconciled, cohesive society? He likened it to a pot that had been broken into numerous small pieces. How do you put them back together again to make a whole, functional pot?

He saw the role of the church as picking up those pieces one by one and, by the grace of God, putting them together. There would be no quick fix. It would be slow, painstaking work, but there was no other way. As he commented, no university could train a person to do such work; it was only through the grace of the Holy Spirit's power that such a miracle is possible. He saw this challenge as his contribution to both the church and the country.

When Kolini arrived in Rwanda, he did not know the church personnel, and they did not know him. The first task was to make a path of dialogue with all the staff. They needed to reconsider their positions in the church and feel confident that they were called by the Lord to the positions they were in. It would be no good if the church had people in leadership positions just because they wanted a job but were not true believers called to service.

The next question that the church personnel needed to ask themselves was, What is my obligation as an individual, and what should we do as a group, for the recovery of our country?

The country and church needed people to be motivated to start working at once toward reconciliation. There was room for outside agencies to help, but the church could not sit back and rely on this. It had an obligation to start work within itself. Even answering these questions took time, for both the church and the country had many biased, angry, prejudiced people. During our conversation, Kolini looked up at me and grinned, "God has been teaching me in the school of sociology these past ten years!"

Following his appointment as archbishop, Kolini was very aware that he was in the middle of two camps: those who supported his ministry and those who had not wanted him to come and were against him. After six months in office he knew he had to address the situation. He told all the leadership and congregations that he was not on one side or the other, but he was called to be bishop to them all and was in office to serve the Lord.

Even after his statement it took some time for people to realize that the country desperately had need of the church at this time and that a divided, prejudiced church was no help to anyone. How could the church fulfill its prophetic role to the nation if it was always arguing? For example, a certain priest had appointed himself to be the dean of the St. Etienne Cathedral, and Kolini had to remove him from office even though he was a man of some considerable influence. It took time for Kolini to win people over and then reunite them because it meant there had to be discipline within his own diocese. He had to put his house in order before it could have a witness to those outside the church. To do this was neither easy nor popular.

New bishops had to be elected and enthroned, for only the bishop of Byumba had returned to his diocese. Even in this there were tensions, and people were watching to see if this new, "foreign" archbishop could put together a team that would work together. After a while, three of the bishops decided to leave—the bishops of Kigeme, Shyogwe, and Butare. It was like history repeating itself. Would the divisions and church politics never be healed? Then while the whole church was feeling insecure, government officials challenged Kolini, wanting to know what was going on. This made the internal church conflict a political problem that spread even further, causing strained relationships with Archbishop Carey of Canterbury. The Mothers' Union withdrew its support from Rwanda at this critical time when it was desperately needed, and the final disaster was that the bishop of Kibungo had personal problems and deserted his flock.[1]

Kolini was then left with all these dioceses to run, as well as his own diocese of Kigali, in addition to the work of the primacy. It meant traveling all over Rwanda to oversee priests and encourage the people. But, in fact, this proved to be a great opportunity to really get to know the country, the people, and the church. Even though Satan and his workers may have been trying to orchestrate Kolini's downfall, the Lord turned it around for good.

The history of the Anglican province had been fractured ever since it was created in 1992, so Kolini focused two-thirds of his time to reestablish and help it function in a way that would support the dioceses. The other third was given to his international duties, because during these years the North American Anglican crisis had also been erupting and shaking the worldwide Anglican Communion. Although at this stage Kolini did not become actively involved in helping the dissidents, he was one of the two primates who consecrated the so-called rebel bishops and, by doing this, alienated himself from ECUSA (the Episcopal Church in the USA). This act cut off the Rwandan Anglican Church from receiving any financial aid from them, and funding was also withdrawn from the Theological Education by Extension program, which was so valuable for training priests and for building provincial offices.

The Lord spoke to him about this and asked, "Do you worship God or money?" His response was immediate: "Lord, I worship you, and I leave you to take care of the rest."

Building Trust

For the past ten years or so Kolini has been seeking to build trust within the Anglican Church and also trust between church and community. There have been many social challenges to address in the aftermath of genocide. Society as a whole has been in a state of denial, suffering from inertia and a guilty conscience. Survivors of the genocide are often full of resentment and fear, and there is mistrust among the different social groups. It took him a long time to even begin to understand how the people around him were thinking and feeling, but without that understanding it would not have been possible to bring a message relevant to the situation. If the church does not bring a relevant message, then it is no use saying, "Never again!" because the "never again" will just happen in another form. This is the way Kolini views his work in Rwanda, and he still constantly asks himself if he really understands and if the message he preaches is really relevant.

In 2005 survivors in his diocese were still being killed just because they were Tutsi. The ethnic divide was there under a thin veil of so-called unity. Kolini needed to ask himself some hard questions: What kind of diocese do I have when there are still killings all around? Do I love these people? Do I preach as an evangelist? Do we, as a church, believe in hell and heaven? If we don't bring a clear message, where will these people go? These questions drove him to his knees, and the Lord gave Kolini a word from Daniel's prophecy (Daniel 9:27; 11:31; 12:11) that the Lord spoke about in Matthew 24:15: "So when you see standing in the holy place 'the abomination that causes desolation,' spoken of through the prophet Daniel—let the reader understand."

Then the Lord showed Kolini four holy places, created by the Holy One, in Rwanda that contained abominations:

- the nation
- the church
- the family
- the individual

The devastating abomination is hatred, and no one could deny the presence of hatred in Rwanda.

Kolini began to challenge his people about holiness. When he would ask people in a congregation if they believed they had been created in God's image, everyone would answer a resounding, "Yes!" He would then ask, "What does that mean? Is God male or female, white or black, Tutsi or Hutu?" They would reply, "No!" He would then say, "We know that God is love, and that is the one attribute that God will share with us, an attribute that he wants us all to have. The image of God that we carry is love. We have seen what happened in this land when love wasn't there! It is never too late to recover, but we need to accept that there is a devastating abomination—hatred—standing in the holy place, in my heart, my family, my church, and my nation. We have to go down on our knees before God in repentance and ask him to wash our image, to make us our true selves, that is, Christ in us and we in him."

In trying to bring this message to the shattered church in Rwanda, in his imagination Kolini saw himself as a general who had taken his troops into battle and lost many of them to the enemy, even though he had survived. What shame to return home without your troops. A good general would go to war and have as few casualties as possible. If it looked as if he was losing the battle, he would withdraw in order to save his soldiers. Kolini saw his role as going to war against the enemy and not losing anyone in the battle, so that one day he can stand before the Lord and say, "Thank you, Lord, for your help; here are your people!" This is the task of a true shepherd.

Shepherding the Shepherds

Much of Kolini's work as bishop of Kigali as well as archbishop of the province has been to work with the priests and pastors. He told them that they must warn people of their spiritual peril, for if they fail to do this, then the blood of their parishioners will be on their hands. If the clergy preach every

Sunday and the people go home without the Word changing their lives, then they have failed in their ministry. The priests and catechists must challenge the congregation; otherwise, the people will think that all is well with their souls when it is not. In most congregations there are many prodigal sons and daughters, and challenging them is a blessing for them; not to do so is equivalent to cursing them.

To be a minister of the gospel in a complex and difficult situation, as exists in Rwanda, is also painful. Kolini has found it lonely as he has endeavored to fulfill a prophetic ministry in his position as archbishop. Often he has felt misunderstood and isolated, but he has been willing to walk in the way that God has shown and led him. He has sought to allow the loneliness to blossom into solitude, which is a very different emotion—one that is positive rather than negative, one that brings no bitterness.

It was a great step forward when the new house of bishops covenanted together never again to allow quarreling and divisions to occur among them, such as had so badly damaged the church in previous years. They promised to tolerate each other and to work together as a team. The Mothers' Union of Rwanda developed a program whereby they visited all the dioceses, and this brought more unity within the province. Choirs began to cross the diocesan borders and visit each other's groups.

There was a constant question posed by politicians: "Are you any different from your brothers and sisters who remained silent about the genocide or who actively took part in it?" It was in this context that Kolini felt, when he was enthroned as the archbishop, a need to apologize publicly to the nation on behalf of the Anglican Church for its failure during the years leading up to and including the genocide of 1994.

He said, "It's not because I was not here that I make myself an innocent. Those who were involved did it on my behalf because they were the church leaders and we belong to the same church. Therefore on behalf of the Anglican Church, I do apologize."

Kolini was the first church leader in the country from any denomination to make an apology, and it had a huge impact on the nation. He also stated clearly that the Anglican Church was not going to repeat the mistakes of the past and continue fighting against the Catholic Church; neither would there be fighting within their own denomination or between Christians and Muslims. This public statement was an important step to take, for the church had publicly been shamed by its failures in the past. Kolini preached on the message of Nehemiah about rebuilding the walls of Jerusalem, the walls of love and righteousness and truth.

How could this be done? There were still enemies who wanted to prevent the church from being rebuilt. The church had to look at the broken walls and clean the debris before it could reuse the stones and start to rebuild. That cleaning process would be internal, each one looking at his or her own life and allowing the Lord to change the individual. Personal, internal change is always a painful procedure. It means an acknowledgement of failure leading to confession and repentance, not a very popular message to give to any generation. By the saving grace of the gospel, it is possible for the church to be cleaned and restored. And it must be done; otherwise, the church cannot survive. The workers also need to pick up their spiritual weapons as they work, for there is always a spiritual battle going on. It is an ongoing challenge.

The renewal of the church is a process that naturally takes time. There are many physical needs to be met within the community, especially among the widows, orphans, returnees, survivors, and released prisoners. All of these groups of people are the responsibility of the church; they are individual stones that need cleaning and rebuilding into the wall.

CHAPTER 15

Reconciliation Initiatives

I n 1999 the Rwandese government was facing a crisis. There were at least 120,000 prisoners held in a few inadequate detention centers.[1] The conditions were appalling, as these prisons were never built to house such vast numbers of people. In some prisons the overcrowding was so intense that there was no room for prisoners to lie down on the floor to sleep. Some even developed gangrene and needed amputations. International pressure was increasing, requiring measures to change the situation.

The first step that the government took was to release the minors, the elderly, and the sick prisoners back into the community. This in itself caused a problem for the victims' relatives and survivors of the genocide. How should the community react to this new challenge? Kolini felt that the church should be involved and take a lead in helping the reconciliation process forward. He invited the Catholics, Protestants, and Muslims, along with politicians and elders of the society, to meet together. He organized a four-day seminar to look at how justice could be served and these prisoners be reintegrated into the society.

Inter-Church Aid[2] helped to finance a successful project that continued for three years. Unfortunately, it then had to be terminated, not because the program didn't work, but because the coordinator embezzled the funds, and it completely destroyed people's faith in the initiative. It had taken those three years to build trust and overcome fear among the main groups of people. The first part of the project had been to train a group of Christian and Muslim workers in the vision of reintegrating Christian and Muslim prisoners back into the community and preparing the community to receive them.

Seminars were organized first for the survivors, then for the prisoners, and finally for the families of prisoners. Kolini had thought that the last two groups might have been easier to manage and have more in common, but it did not prove to be the case. For five long days the groups worked together, prayed together, and listened together. Then the groups discussed together.

The first seminars were very difficult. The survivors could not tolerate being near the prisoners and would not sleep in the same dormitory blocks or eat at the same tables. Some of the participants just relied on the organizers, not really wanting to work on issues for themselves. After a few months the people were recalled for a follow-up seminar, and it was encouraging to see different attitudes and the groups beginning to eat together and accept each other.

Kolini told me the story of one woman. She was a very angry and traumatized woman who was a survivor of the genocide. Whenever this woman saw a Hutu, her emotions overwhelmed her. At one of these seminars she encountered a man who was not only a Hutu but also a former soldier, and she suffered a serious trauma. She received counseling and support from her pastor, and, eventually, at the second seminar she was able to sit at the same table and eat with this man. They shared their pain together, and trust began to build. By the time they met at a third seminar they were able to share in dancing and hugging each other. This couple eventually became engaged and married, even though their families did not understand or approve. Reconciliation can be real.

This was typical of what happened during the seminars. People turned from hating and shunning each other to listening to each other's pain. From words sprang actions as they ate together, slept in the same dormitories, and learned to dance and sing together. There were also projects that involved practical work together—things like grinding millet and corn and helping to provide shelter—all aimed at rebuilding the community.

There was some money available to build houses for those most in need. It was not possible to do this for everybody, but the community helped those who were in the most desperate situations. Altogether there were about five hundred people from the three groups: survivors, prisoners, and prisoners' families. There was only enough money to build 150 small homes.

In one area there was a young woman who was a survivor, and she was working with another woman who was the wife of a man still in prison. He was imprisoned because he had killed the family of that same young woman. The house of the prisoner's wife was in a terrible condition and needed much repair to make it habitable. The young woman had been given new iron sheets (corrugated roofing sheets) to repair her leaky roof, but when she saw the terrible conditions this other woman lived in, she gave the iron sheets to her as she felt her needs were greater. It was an amazing testimony of reconciliation.

This project ran well and was a real challenge for both Christians and Muslims to show that they could work together for the good of their country. Out of the positive effects of this project sprang another interfaith initiative, which was later linked to the Conference for World Peace.[3]

In 2005 there was a conference hosted in Rwanda during which Muslims and Christians met together to discuss how they could be instruments for peace and reconciliation, not just nationally but globally. In our world today where so much antagonism is in evidence between Muslim and Christian communities, Kolini has been encouraged by what has been achieved in Rwanda through friendship and dialogue, and his hope is that this will grow and benefit not only Rwanda but also the rest of the world.

CHAPTER 16

Helping the
Sick and Needy

One of the qualifications that supported Kolini when he was invited to go to Rwanda to serve as bishop of Kigali was his interest in the problem of HIV/AIDS. While serving the church in Congo, he had sought to become informed about the disease, as it was an ever-increasing problem. In 1990 he was invited to go to Canada, and during that visit he was able to see how a Christian center and hospice was meeting the needs of people in the terminal stages of the illness. It impressed him deeply and reinforced his view that the church should be involved and ministering God's grace in the AIDS epidemic sweeping sub-Saharan Africa in such an alarming way.

After his visit to Canada, Kolini began an HIV-awareness campaign in his diocese in Congo. He was able to borrow some songs on tape that had been made by a Ugandan musician named Rutaya, solely to bring the message to the average person in a way that would be understood and received. Then he was able to work within the research center sponsored by the United States Agency for International Development (USAID) in Congo. All this gave him understanding and experience so that when the Rwandese government was trying to set up an AIDS commission after the genocide, they asked Kolini if he would be the national chairman. He took the post and led the work for five years. It was a project in which all the churches were happy to cooperate, along with the Muslim community; so once again, it became an interfaith venture.

The work of this commission has been part of the reason for the encouraging fall in the statistics of HIV/AIDS within the population of Rwanda, from 10 to 11 percent after the genocide to 3 percent in 2007.

Kolini's part in this was to acquire a large grant from the World Bank, which entailed the hard work of preparing the project proposals and presenting them to the bank so that eventually a grant of 32 million US dollars was released. Although Kolini is no longer the chairman of the commission, the community, church, and government are continuing to work together to defeat a common enemy. HIV doesn't recognize the boundaries of ethnicity, religion, or denomination.

I (Mary) remember visiting a small mud-brick church one Sunday morning. We left Kigali and traveled for some distance on the tarmac road but then turned off and wound our way on a dusty, bumpy track for several miles until we reached a rather remote village. I was due to preach at the morning service, but once this was over, we had a short break before a group of people began gathering again in the church. It was the support group for the members of the congregation who knew they were infected with HIV/AIDS. I sat in the meeting and was very impressed by the helpful discussions.

After the meeting we met with another group of young people who were hoping to get married, and the pastor was encouraging them to all get tested for HIV/AIDS before marriage. The tests were free, and the pastor told them that he had been one of the first to go for the test when it became available. He tried to impress on his listeners that there was no shame in taking the test. It did not mean that a person was admitting to being promiscuous, but rather it was just a sensible precaution. I could see amazement on the faces of the young people as they learned that HIV/AIDS could be spread through dirty needles or infected blood transfusions. I was very impressed at the health education given by the church in that village.

When the meetings were all over, I accompanied the pastor to a hospital some considerable distance away where one of his parishioners was being treated for AIDS. We entered the ward, which was exclusively for AIDS patients, and the woman we had come to visit was lying in the end bed. It was obvious she was very sick. We prayed together and read the Scriptures. The pastor's wife had brought a gift of food. Then we went along the row of beds, and the pastor talked to all the patients, although they were not his parishioners. My heart was deeply moved as I saw this demonstration of Christ's love to these needy people.

I had witnessed love in action in one small parish within the Kigali diocese, engaging the church in the problem of HIV.

Kolini has found that his involvement with the AIDS commission has taught him even more about human nature. It amazes him to think that once people are educated about the way this killer disease is transmitted, they still do not take the steps required to stop it from spreading. Why hasn't it died out within months or even a year? What is it within human nature that is able to disregard knowledge and carry on with sexual promiscuity?

The apostle Paul stated in Romans 7:14–25: "I know what I am supposed to do and I am wanting to do that; but whenever I try to do it, I find I am doing wrong! I don't do the right which I had planned to do. Oh, who can save me from this body of death?" (paraphrased by Kolini).

As he explained, the force within us goes beyond our logical thinking and makes us vulnerable. Only the cross of Christ and the grace of God can give us strength to overcome this human weakness. This is why it is so important to give the gospel message to people as well as to help them in their need. We have to understand the human weakness that we all carry and not be judgmental of those who are infected with HIV/AIDS.

After the genocide many children were left without any adult relatives to care for them and had nowhere to live. Often, an older child would gather younger siblings or friends and take care of them. They might live in an abandoned building or even out in the bush, scavenging food or harvesting from abandoned gardens. These are children looking after children and are known in the country as child-headed families, or CHFs. They are another group of needy people who are a great challenge for the church and with whom the archbishop has been actively involved.

Within the Kigali diocese two villages have been built with the help of British missions to provide safe houses for these youngsters. The village at Ruhanga is well established, and the children are sponsored so that they are able to complete their education, if that is appropriate, or begin vocational training courses. The archdeacon looks after their spiritual welfare and a social worker, their material needs. A similar village at nearby Kabuga, called Hope Village, is partially constructed, with a number of children able to live in that safe environment.

Kolini was also challenged about the plight of the prisoners. He realized that whatever they had done, they had spiritual needs. He remembered our Lord's words that he spoke as a rebuke in the parable of the sheep and the goats: "I was sick and in prison and you did not look after me" (Matthew 25:31–46).

Kolini began to visit prisons and encouraged his priests to do the same. They found prisoners ready to receive the gospel and turn from their sin to trust in Jesus. Many confirmations were held within the prison walls. He was able to invite Prison Fellowship International[1] to come to Rwanda and help with the ministry. It has been a successful partnership and helpful in the reconciliation ministry. The story of one of the priests who has been greatly used in prison work, Stephen Gahigi, himself a survivor of genocide, is told in my book *After Genocide—There Is Hope.*[2]

Archbishop Kolini's ministry is reaching out not only to groups of needy people but also to individuals who need his help. One such individual was a Scottish woman who was widowed during the genocide.

Lesley Bilinda was a missionary with Tearfund[3] who had gone to Rwanda in 1989 to serve at Gahini as a coordinator of a community health project. Within a very short time after her arrival she had fallen in love with the country and its warm-hearted people. She lived with a Rwandan family while she settled in and learned the language and became like a daughter to her hosts. After a while, she fell in love again. This time it was with one of the young Rwandan pastors, the Reverend Charles Bilinda. Charles was an English teacher in the local church secondary school, and it was great for Lesley to have someone she could speak English with. They were married, and their home was in Gahini when the genocide began. Lesley had gone for a short vacation to Kenya with her sister who was visiting from Scotland when President Habyarimana's plane was shot down and the genocide started. She was desperate to get news of her husband, Charles. The situation was so terrible that she was unable to return to Rwanda for several months. All the information she had managed to obtain during that time indicated that her husband had been killed at Butare. When she returned to Rwanda, she learned for certain that he was dead, but there was no one who was able to give her a clear story of what had happened. In desperation and distress Lesley returned to Scotland to grieve. In time she set up a trust in memory of Charles to help Rwandans obtain further education.

Ten years after the genocide, Lesley returned to Rwanda, having agreed to make a film of her experiences and also trying to find out what really happened to Charles. It was an emotionally painful trip for her as she struggled to come to terms with facts that were emerging through the investigations.

One day while she was in Kigali, she asked to see Archbishop Kolini for a few moments. Although he was very busy in a bishop's court, he slipped out from the meeting and met her in the Kigali Cathedral parking lot. Lesley later spoke of how warmly Kolini greeted her, not just with the customary Rwandese hug, but holding her in a fatherly embrace. He talked to her and prayed with her about her pain and distress. The prayer so touched her heart that she began to weep, her tears flowing freely onto Kolini's jacket. She was overwhelmed by his tenderness and pastoral care. It didn't matter that she was a foreigner and, in terms of loss, had probably suffered less than so many Rwandese. Kolini understood and cared about her pain and prayed about her problem. She said she would never forget his kindness to her in her hour of need, sparing time from a very important meeting to greet her and pray with her.

CHAPTER 17

A Pastor to the North American Brethren

As has been explained elsewhere in this book, leadership brings inevitable conflicts when decisions have to be made that are controversial. Leadership by its very nature can bring loneliness and isolation. This has been very much the case for Kolini in recent years, as he has sought to help some of the North American Anglicans who made an appeal to the Anglican world to help them in their dilemma. His response to that appeal was to try to address the theological issues of the uniqueness of Christ, the authority of the Scriptures, and centrality of the cross to deal with our sin; and he also shared the lessons of his life experience.

Kolini had fled to Uganda as a refugee. When he arrived, no one asked him, "Where is your passport? Do you have a criminal record?" He was received just as a person in dire need of refuge. How do you repay that sort of kindness? In Rwandese culture if even an animal is hurt and comes into a house for refuge, it is never turned away. It is an obligation for the household to provide refuge for people or even animals that appeal for help.

So when Kolini heard in his spirit the cry for help from his distressed North American brothers and sisters, his immediate response was, "The Lord gave me a safe place of refuge; why should I deny it to others?"

He also remembers, only too clearly, that when Rwanda cried out to the rest of the world for help, the rest of the world did not listen. What the world did to his country, Kolini, as a Christian, prays he will never inflict on anyone else. He knew he had to open his arms and welcome these brothers and sisters by accepting them and trying to help them.

There was no discussion as to whether or not they were "real" Anglicans; it was just a fact of hearing "a cry in the desert" that needed a positive response. Someone was in danger; it was as if their house was burning down and they needed a place of shelter. Later when theological issues were discussed, Kolini realized that these people were also brothers and sisters at a deeper theological level.

Through his involvement with the North American church, Kolini has found that by receiving other people in this way, some of his past experiential pain can become their blessing, and this has also given him joy.

When Kolini felt that he had lost everything as a refugee— his home, country, education, and prospects—his life was very painful. Yet, through that experience he learned to see that God, who created the world out of nothing, could take our nothingness and by his grace help us to start over again and enable us to work to create something new. God reminded him of the story of Hagar, who had lost everything. When she cried to God, he heard her cry in the desert and provided a fresh spring of water. That is exactly what God did in the Kinyara refugee camp where people were literally dying all around him. The Lord brought joy and hope right in the middle of death. Spiritual life was born and with it a strength to work.

So Kolini became involved with AMiA, the acronym by which the Anglican Mission in the Americas is known. No doubt there will be many readers who know all about the mission, but for others I will endeavor to explain a little of the history and work of this organization.

The great missionary movements of the nineteenth and early twentieth centuries sprang mainly from the church in Europe and North America. These continents were experiencing a growth in church life and a commitment to the truth of the Word of God that resulted in a drive to take the gospel to every land, thus fulfilling Christ's Great Commission of Matthew 28:18–20. Intrepid missionaries took the gospel to every corner of the globe, facing dangers and threats that would astonish people of this present generation. They carried the gospel to far-flung areas of Africa and Asia, never dreaming that the time would come when missionaries from these continents would need to bring it back to the homelands, because the church had strayed so far from the truth. Now, in the twenty-first century, "the U.S. is now home to the largest population of un-churched and spiritually disconnected English-speaking people in the world, who are searching for true meaning and significance."[1]

In North American churches membership is declining steadily, and nominalism and liberalism are rife within the Anglican Church. Throughout the Christian world, homosexuality, being both practiced and accepted within the leadership of the church in North America, has caused distress and concern, especially to the evangelical wing of the church. Many basic truths of the faith have been abandoned, and the authority of the Scriptures undermined. It is no wonder that confused people are deserting the faith of their forefathers and leaving the church. The individual congregations that wanted to stay true to the teachings of the Bible were left with a huge dilemma. How could they remain in the Anglican Communion while staying true to their consciences and faithful to the Word of God? They loved the Anglican tradition and did not want to leave it.

If the church in the West was declining, the opposite was happening in many other parts of the world. Some continents were experiencing an incredible explosion of Christian growth, with churches crowded to the door, holding several services each Sunday to accommodate the thousands who wanted to worship. Churches in Africa, Asia, and South America have been experiencing a wonderful time of blessing and revival in recent years. These areas are often referred to collectively as "the Global South," and the vibrant churches in these areas have taken up the baton of spreading the gospel throughout the world.

In 2000 Archbishop Kolini, together with Archbishop Moses Tay from the province of Southeast Asia, came to the aid of some of the struggling members of the Episcopal Church in North America by establishing a missionary organization, the Anglican Mission in America. It was formalized on July 28, 2000, in Amsterdam and charged with a commission to preach the gospel and make disciples in North America through church planting.

The two archbishops consecrated the Reverend Charles Murphy and the Reverend John Rogers to serve as missionary bishops. Bishop Murphy belongs to the house of bishops in Rwanda and is responsible to Archbishop Kolini, and Bishop Rogers is responsible to the archbishop of Southeast Asia. Both work in an outreach capacity in the United States.

The following year in Denver, Archbishop Tay's successor, Archbishop Yong Ping Chung, along with Archbishop Kolini, consecrated four more bishops, and so the new movement began to grow and become established. The AMiA solved the dilemma of the evangelicals who sincerely wished to remain within the Episcopal Church in North America, yet also remain true to both the teachings of the Scriptures and the Thirty-nine Articles of the Anglican Church.

As the movement has developed and grown, so the core values have also become crystallized. They are summarized as being the Scriptures, the Spirit, and the Sacred. These three core values are seen as three streams flowing from one great river. It is a river of life and healing that transforms individuals, communities, and countries.

The Scriptures

The focus on the Scriptures is in accordance with the evangelical tradition of the church that emphasizes the authority of Scripture as God's Holy Word, divinely inspired and containing all that is needed for salvation and discipleship. It is the final authority in all matters of faith and practice. It also emphasizes the need to proclaim the gospel to the human race, bringing to the attention of the hearers the need for a personal relationship with God through the redemptive work of Jesus Christ on the cross of Calvary and through his resurrection. This is achieved as the church reaches out to the world in evangelism and mission. These beliefs are based on the two Scriptures: 2 Timothy 3:16–17 and John 3:16.

The Spirit

The work of the Holy Spirit within the church of God is acknowledged and celebrated, a focus often associated with the charismatic movement within the church. The Anglican Mission believes that God's Holy Spirit was poured out on the infant church at Pentecost and has continued to be poured out on believers through the generations, even to this day, transforming the lives of Christians and demonstrating the power of God through signs and wonders to the unbelieving world. The Holy Spirit distributes spiritual gifts to all believers to guide, teach, and equip them for service. These beliefs are founded on key Scriptures: Luke 24:49; Acts 1:8; and 1 Corinthians 12.

The Sacred

The Anglican Mission also has a strong belief in the sacramental life of the church and its historic faith. It believes in what the 1662 Prayer Book describes as the "One Holy, Catholic and Apostolic church." This church has taught and adhered to the Apostles' and Nicene Creeds and the Thirty-nine Articles of religion. This is the faith handed down from our forefathers, the faith for which the saints of old were tortured and burned at the stake.

In recent generations many have denied the truths for which these saints fought and gave their lives. The American Mission values the heritage of the Anglican Church as expressed in the prayer books of the sixteenth and seventeenth centuries. It values the structure of worship and the theological standing that transcend national traditions and boundaries.

With these values at its center, the Anglican Mission in America has flourished, receiving into its membership existing congregations that were unable, in good conscience, to continue in membership with the existing Episcopal Church of America. The AMiA has also planted new churches in the United States. The work has now spread beyond the national boundaries and includes fellowships from Canada, Portugal, and Puerto Rico. It is growing at such a rate that, on average, a new church is added to its ranks every three weeks.

At the request of Archbishop Kolini in 2007, the Anglican Mission has expanded to become an umbrella organization incorporating the Anglican Mission in America, the Anglican

Coalition of Canada, and the Anglican Coalition in America. It is now known as the Anglican Mission in the Americas. This organization not only covers the two countries of the United States and Canada but also embraces their two positions on the ordination of women. The AMiA ordains women only to the deaconate, whereas the other two organizations ordain women into the priesthood, as does the Anglican Church of Rwanda.

Many people mistakenly think that the reason why the churches in the United States have affiliated with the province of Rwanda is because of the attitudes toward homosexuality tolerated within the mainstream Episcopal Church in the United States, but I hope that this explanation of the birth of the Anglican Mission shows that the issues are far wider than that one alone.

The Anglican Mission is not a breakaway movement as such; it is simply realignment in terms of leadership in which the bishops are accountable to Archbishop Kolini and the house of bishops within the province of Rwanda, which in its own right is a full member of the Anglican Communion. The bishops who have been consecrated as missionary bishops to the United States have all been consecrated in accordance with the constitution and canons of the province of Rwanda.

Some people have questioned that bishops have come under the authority of provinces that are so far away from them geographically. In an interesting response to the Windsor Report in 2005, Archbishop Kolini along with the Most Reverend Fidele Dirokpa of Congo, the Most Reverend Bernard Malango of Central Africa, the Most Reverend Benjamin Nzimbi of Kenya, and the Most Reverend Yong Ping Chung of Southeast Asia have very ably demonstrated from Scripture and early church history that this is not a new phenomenon, but in fact has been practiced on many occasions in different places as the need arose. For centuries it has been an accepted way of maintaining purity of doctrine and vibrant faith within the church.

In 1 Peter 3:15–16 we read, "Always be prepared to give an answer to everyone who asks you to give the reason for the hope that you have. But do this with gentleness and respect, keeping a clear conscience." It is not easy to stand against a majority for the sake of your conscience, yet this is what Kolini has been able to do, even though it has made him unpopular within some ranks of the Anglican Communion. His position has often been misunderstood and even ridiculed. It reminds me of William Wilberforce who worked so hard and was much ridiculed and misunderstood in the British parliament as he campaigned for the abolition of the slave trade. He was a Christian who was true to his conscience despite personal cost, and so is Emmanuel Kolini in our generation. He and his colleagues have taken such a stand to preserve the truth of doctrine and theology of the church.

CHAPTER 18

Thank God for People!

Whittps://hen Kolini reflects on his life, he frequently comments not only on how the Lord has kept him in safety but also on how often other leaders have positively impacted his life. Although he has never had the privilege of meeting the great evangelist Billy Graham, he realizes that this man's writing has influenced his life and thinking. When Kolini was in Burundi, training for ordination, he was given the job of college librarian. This gave him opportunity to read many books. He remembers reading Graham's *Peace with God* as a young Christian and being very blessed by it. It made the gospel so clear to him. He also read Graham's biography and has never forgotten the passage describing him sitting by a river and preaching to the fish. When the young Graham realized that if he made an altar call, there would be no response, he decided he had better start preaching to people. Billy Graham's commitment to preaching the whole gospel at every opportunity resonated with Kolini's own desire.

In 1959 when he was still a boy at the Catholic secondary school in Nyundo, there was a bishop who truly was a man of God filled with the Holy Spirit. He was the very first Rwandan bishop, and his name was Aloys Bigirumwami. As a pupil, when he was still a practicing Roman Catholic, Kolini was a server for him at the altar. At the Pentecost service, he was sitting very near the pulpit when this man was preaching. The bishop said very clearly, "I am a Christian, and God knows it!" That phrase kept coming into Kolini's mind and challenging him.

Also in 1959 during the ethnic troubles when houses were being burned, Bigirumwami would be out very early in the morning, trying to help and comfort his people. He really looked after the people in his diocese. The story is told that one day he came across a goat whose leg had been slashed by a machete. Sometimes people were sadistic and thought nothing of hurting animals. Such was his compassion that he got out of his car and found some bandages and cared for the goat's wounds. This story illustrated the loving heart this bishop had, and it was an inspiration to Kolini.

Bigirumwami's life was not an easy one. He was a Tutsi and had many problems with the leadership within his diocese because of this. A great number of the priests under his care were killed during the massacres, and those who remained behind were working against him. However, through it all he maintained a tremendous witness. He was Rwandese and took his Christianity into the Rwandan context. He wrote a book about the gospel and culture, which was a great help to many people who were struggling with the Catholic Church being a tool of colonialism. He had not been afraid to challenge the *muzungu* Bishop Perrodin of Kabgayi, who ran away and deserted his diocese. Bigirumwami sent him a letter warning him that he had forgotten his calling.

Even President Habyarimana respected him because Bigirumwami had helped him during his school days. He was a truly remarkable man, one of God's saints. Kolini recalls the day he died; it rained hard, even though it was the July–August dry season. (Rain is considered to be a sign of God's blessing in Rwanda.) When so many Catholic priests had disillusioned Kolini with God, this man stood out as one who truly pointed the way to the Lord.

Another priest who has influenced Kolini by his stand for truth is Bishop Ngabu of Goma. He, too, was a Roman Catholic bishop who fought for justice during the difficult days of the Mobutu regime in Congo. One day the president sent word to Ngabu that he was coming to Mass, but he didn't come. Some time later the president invited Ngabu to supper, but he refused to go. His answer to the president was, "No, thank you. So long as you do not come for Mass, then I am not coming to you for supper!"

It was an incredibly brave thing to say to the president, who was virtually a dictator and did not like being crossed. From then on he was a marked man. One day the militia tried to kill him by throwing a grenade inside the church. Even to this day,

Bishop Ngabu stands up and speaks out for the marginalized in his diocese and country, and for this Kolini admires him.

Festo Kivengere is another Christian for whom Kolini has a great respect. One of his most vivid memories of this courageous man was during the regime of Idi Amin in Uganda. Archbishop Janani Luwum had been brutally murdered, and Festo went to retrieve his body to bring it to Namirembe Cathedral for burial. When Festo went to ask for the body, Amin became angry and said, "Go away from me, or I may kill you!" Festo replied, "You may kill Kivengeri, but you cannot kill Festo, because Festo believes in Jesus, who died and rose again and lives in him. Therefore, Festo will never die, because Jesus will never die again. But if you, Amin, will not believe in Jesus, you will die forever!"

Amin was furious and ordered him to leave. On the way home Festo had to change cars because his home was six hours away. Once home, he found that the security forces had been several times to the house, looking for him. Festo called the church leaders for prayer, and the leaders begged him to leave. At first he refused but eventually agreed to cross the border into Rwanda for his own safety, going by the Panya route, which means not crossing at the border custom controls.

Festo had been converted in 1941when he was the assistant headmaster at Kinyasaano School in North Kigezi, Uganda. It was during one of the times of revival that he came to Christ, and he remained faithful to the teachings of the *balokole* (revival movement) all through his long life. He progressed in his career in education, becoming the school supervisor for the Church of Uganda. He is, however, most remembered for his faithful ministry as a priest and bishop in the Church of Uganda. Festo loved singing and was largely responsible for deciding that new hymns should be collected and added to the church hymnbook, including Ugandan and Rwandan songs, rather than just hymns imported from abroad.

He also had a heart for preaching the gospel, and in 1969 he undertook a preaching tour of all the CMS Rwanda Mission stations in Rwanda and Burundi, holding evangelistic meetings. The Lord blessed his endeavors with many coming to faith. Following the death of Archbishop Luwum in 1977, Festo, for his own safety, had to leave Uganda, eventually traveling to North America where he lived in exile. While he was in the United States, a reporter once asked him, "If you were given a gun and were sitting with Amin, what would you do?" Festo replied, "I would hand the gun to Amin; my hope is in the Bible." In 1977 he was awarded the International Freedom Prize in Oslo, for his stand on freedom and human rights.

Kolini, too, has such a heart for preaching the gospel, and men like Festo Kivengere and Bishop Rwakaikara—who like Festo preached the gospel of salvation through the blood of Jesus—have all been an inspiration to him.

When Kolini began his parish ministry in Bunyoro, he also learned a great deal from his third bishop there. Bishop Yustace Ruhindi was not the stickler for tradition in the same way many Ugandan bishops were, although he was a true Anglican. He could see when traditions were hindering the gospel and was willing to be flexible in order to reach people. One of the things he was willing to do was to baptize the children of women who had only had a tribal wedding and not a church wedding. This was very much against the traditions of the church, but was a means of bringing the gospel and the grace of God to his people. Working under him taught Kolini to see the difference between mere tradition and biblical truth. It was a lesson that proved invaluable when he served in Congo.

The archbishop he served under in Congo was another inspiration to him. This man, Ndahura, was a beloved pastor to Kolini and Freda, and he worked so hard giving his whole life to serve his church. When Ndahura had been a young man, the legendary African missionary Apollo of the Pygmies had performed a miracle on him. Ndahura had become sick and died, and Apollo stretched himself on the young man just as Elisha had done on a boy in the Old Testament. Ndahura had revived and lived to serve the Lord. His request is that at the end of his days he would be buried alongside Apollo.

Another inspiring example of an African archbishop for Kolini has been Samuel Sindamuka, the former archbishop of Burundi. When this man was only nineteen years old, he walked alone all the way from Burundi to Kabale to attend the *balokole* convention and then walked back. Not only was it three hundred miles, but also wild animals still lived in the bush. Such was his hunger for God and to know revival in his own heart that he was willing to make this journey.

Samuel was greatly respected in Burundi. During times of ethnic fighting between the Hutu and Tutsi, both parties met on his compound, seeking refuge. Both groups of people trusted him, and he hid them all. He was able to travel into rebel areas unmolested in order to take services and confirmations, and all the people would gather and listen to him whatever their ethnic identity because they recognized him as a man of God. He became one of Burundi's first members of parliament, yet as a politician he kept his faith and remained in this office until he was enthroned as archbishop. He challenged his leaders in a godly, gentle way. He was a quiet man, never talking loudly, yet he had such a powerful testimony.

Once Archbishop Sindamuka was in England and was invited to preach in Durham Cathedral. He was instructed to preach for only five minutes because he needed an interpreter. He laughed and said, "When you go to a hotel and they serve you a wonderful meal, do you expect to eat it in five minutes?" "No, of course not!" was the answer the cathedral officials gave him. "So, when you come to have spiritual food, how can you taste it and eat it in five minutes!" he challenged them. Samuel preached for half an hour.

All these men of God inspired and taught Kolini through his life, helping him to learn the lessons he would need for his leadership role within the Anglican Communion, not just in Africa but throughout the world.

Kolini, despite all his commitments, is also a devoted family man. His wife, Freda, has been his best friend and supporter as well as lover, and without her he would not have been able to become the leader he is today. Many times he has been called away because of duties, and his wife and children have understood and released him to do the Lord's work. Family life often had to be sacrificed; this was particularly the case when the children were small and the family was living in Congo. Often Kolini's position required him to make long and arduous journeys on church business, sometimes absent from home for weeks at a time. Nevertheless, Kolini's family is his pride and joy. He inherited his mother's love for children, and each of the nine children born to him and Freda was a welcome and special addition to the family.

There have been times of great sadness for the family as well as times of great joy. Both the firstborn child, Christopher, and the second-born, Jeanette, died and are now with the Lord. Jeanette died when she was just two years old, and her story has been told elsewhere in this book. Christopher died in 2002, as a young husband and father, from spinal cancer. He had been working as a pastor to the street kids in Kigali and was greatly respected and beloved by them. It was a very difficult time for the family. Christopher's wife and little boy, Shema, now live in the Kolini family home, where he can receive the love and care of the grandparents. He is a very bright young lad who is now in nursery school and who loves playing soccer.

Another sadness faced recently was the death of Freda's father, Silas Sibomana, in November 2007, after a long, brave struggle with liver disease. The inspiration of his life and testimony will always be an encouragement to his family.

Emmanuel and Freda's children have all done well in their studies and are a righteous source of pride to their parents. John Haki is at present in Ghana, studying for his master's degree in human resources and working for a Dutch firm there. He has now assumed the responsibility of being the eldest child and son, following the death of Christopher.

Harry (Heri) Peter Umbona is now a lawyer and working for a telecommunications company.

Amani Godfrey graduated in dentistry. He now lives in Kigali, so his parents are able to see him frequently.

Joanna Kira is living in South Africa and is doing environmental studies. She goes by the name Kira. This was the name of her grandmother, the woman from whom Kolini learned his values as a child. When this woman found Christ and was baptized by one of Kolini's priests, the whole village where she was living converted and got baptized.

David Agaba also studied law and is now earning his master's degree in the conflict aspects of international law.

Joy Asisimwe is their next child. Asisimwe means "God be praised." Although she is married and the mother of two small sons, she has followed her brothers' examples and is studying law.

Anna Amara is their youngest child. Her second name has the meaning "Jesus satisfies." Anna has moved to South Africa to continue her studies in social sciences. She has a loving heart for people with problems, just like her parents.

Besides their natural children, Kolini and Freda have raised two orphans: "young" Joy, the daughter of Freda's brother, and Guy, the son of Freda's youngest sister. Two other nephews are in the family: Bob, who has just graduated from finance school, and Junior, who is studying medicine at Rwandan State University.

Life is always busy in the Kolini household, and although Kolini isn't able to be at home as much as he would wish, his family continues to bring him much joy, and he is a much-beloved husband, father, and grandfather.

Frequently, the comment is heard in Christian circles, "God is no man's debtor." Kolini and Freda have made many costly sacrifices during their years of service and mission, and it is so wonderful to see how God has blessed and prospered their family.

CHAPTER 19

The Future

Noone of us can legislate for the future. It remains a sealed book for us all. However, we all have our hopes and dreams, Emmanuel and Freda included. After so many very busy years of faithful service, Kolini looks forward to handing over the responsibility of the province in 2010. I am reminded of the poem "Leisure" by William Henry Davies. Kolini and Freda have had little opportunity to "stand and stare." Perhaps the future years will give this to them.

"Leisure"

> What is this life if, full of care,
> We have no time to stand and stare.

No time to stand beneath the boughs
And stare as long as sheep and cows.

No time to see, when woods we pass,
Where squirrels hide their nuts in grass.

No time to see, in broad daylight
Streams of stars, like skies at night.

No time to turn at Beauty's glance,
And watch her feet, how they can dance.

No time to wait till her mouth can
Enrich that smile her eyes began.

A poor life this, if, full of care,
We have no time to stand and stare.

(William Henry Davies, 1871–1940)

The years of ministry often included traveling all over the world, and many friends have been made, but often there has not been the opportunity to stay long in the company of these friends. As they anticipate their retirement, Emmanuel and Freda hope that with less pressure of work, they will be able to visit and enjoy these friendships. They are also looking forward to spending time with their children and delightful grandsons. One of the deepest pleasures of being part of the older generation is to be able to spend quality time with the family.

Retirement is not an end of work or usefulness. A whole new world opens with endless opportunities. Kolini and Freda have hearts and minds that hunger to discover and grow. Many times Kolini expressed to me that different situations were classrooms to him and that the Lord has been teaching him many lessons. Retirement will be yet another classroom.

Our spiritual journeys continue, and the Lord has work for us to do until we reach the door of heaven. I am reminded of Leonardo da Vinci, the astonishing painter, sculptor, and scientist. He kept journals of all his ideas, and in one he noted, "Iron rusts from disuse; stagnant water loses its purity and in cold weather becomes frozen; even so does inaction sap the vigor of the mind." He continued to make and record discoveries until the very end of his life.

Kolini's mind will not "rust from disuse," and the Lord will continue to use him with his wealth of spirituality and experience to build his church and his people.

The Challenges
of Leadership

O
ne of the most difficult tasks of a leader is to challenge
other people, especially other leaders, about actions that are
unrighteous or unhelpful to the ministry of the gospel. There
have been several times when this has fallen to Kolini's lot, and
he has risen to the challenge.

He recalls that in the 1970s while in Uganda he saw some
of the rigidity and legalistic attitudes of the reawakened brethren
that deeply concerned him. Although he was his junior, Kolini
felt that he had to approach and challenge his much-respected
archdeacon, Ven. Swithin Nyarubona about these matters. His
archdeacon belonged to the reawakened group, but Kolini felt
the life within the church was hindered by the rules this group

had made. So he willingly took a stand, even though he knew it would make him unpopular and he would be misunderstood.

Another occasion when he had to make a stand against his superior occurred while he was assistant bishop in Congo. He needed to disagree with his diocesan bishop, and the bishop gave him such a hard time that he almost resigned. Another priest helped him to be strong and continue, reminding Kolini that if he did resign, it would make the bishop appear to be correct in the matter. Also, if the bishop won that battle, he would gradually impose his will on all the priests, regardless of whether he was right or wrong, and the church would be weakened. With this encouragement, Kolini continued to stand for what he knew was righteous, regardless of the opposition.

This experience prepared Kolini to stand alone in 1987 against all the other bishops in the province over a matter that concerned the late archbishop of Rwanda. He persevered and challenged what he felt to be wrong, despite threats to isolate him and also to report him to the government.

He boldly stood against the threats, stating that he did not and would not separate his faith from the church and that he did not engage in politics. For a year the bishops shunned him, but eventually they realized that what they were doing was wrong, and the relationship was restored. It was a hard year of isolation for his convictions.

Perhaps the most difficult stand of all that Kolini has had to make has been over the AMiA issue. This has necessitated him speaking against the views of both the archbishop of Canterbury and the presiding bishop of America. It has been very difficult to take the risk of isolation and stand for what he has felt was truth; it was a step of faith, controversial and painful. Kolini told me that he had to decide whom he should obey. The Lord reminded him of the Pharisees and the high priest who put Peter and John in prison for preaching the gospel; and when they were charged not to speak in the name of Jesus, they answered, "Judge for yourselves whether it is right in God's sight to obey you rather than God" (Acts 4:19).

The moments of confrontation have been extremely difficult, but Kolini had a choice: Would he compromise his own faith and integrity because he was challenged by someone in higher authority, or would he keep his faith and pay the price?

To stand as a leader who is faithful to his conscience and the truth of God takes courage, and I have no doubt that history will reveal what a significant place Archbishop Kolini has held as a man of God for his generation.

At the Africa Conference held in England in November 2007, Dr. Tokunboh Adeyemo gave a lecture entitled "The Enigma of Africa."

Among his interesting observations, he mentioned that this continent is the richest in the world, yet it has the poorest people. It was the first human home, where the earliest human remains have been discovered, yet it has been the last place to be developed. It is hospitable to others, yet it is very hostile to itself, with constant civil wars.

After elaborating on these enigmas, he then asked, "What is the solution?" He answered his own question that the solution to Africa's problems is to have servant leaders. According to

Adeyemo, Africa needed two types of biblical leaders: *Proistemi* is the Greek word for managers and administrators (Romans 12:8), and *kubernesis* is the Greek word for pioneers and prophetic leaders (1 Corinthians 12:28).

Adeyemo saw anointed leadership involving the following:

- Problem solving
- Provision of goods and services (like Jesus healing and feeding)
- Paving the way for others to follow
- Persuading others (influencing, not dictating)
- Pace setting by example
- Power and presence of God on display
- Paying the ultimate price if called on to do so

Then he commented that such leaders are pioneers, not settlers.

As I was listening to Dr. Adeyemo, I felt as if God were saying to me, "I have leaders like this, leaders like Kolini. Pray for them, and pray that others will be trained to follow in their footsteps. Africa's enigma has a solution!"

My prayer is that Kolini's story will inspire us all to greater faith and to pray for him and those who will follow in his footsteps as servant leaders for Africa's church.

Glossary

I have referred to the country of Congo throughout this book. Many people refer to it as *the* Congo. It was previously known as Belgian Congo until independence, when the name changed to Zaire for several years. Today it is officially known as the Democratic Republic of the Congo.

Ba is the prefix used for people groups, e.g., *Bahutu, Batoro, Batutsi, Batwa.*

Balokole is the term used especially in Uganda for the "saved ones," those touched by the revival.

Duka is a small store found in villages or beside the road.

Imana is the Rwandese word for "the creator God."

Interahamwe is the name taken by the local Hutu extremist militia groups in the genocide. Literally it means "those who attack together."

Intore is the name of the ancient warriors' dance (literally, "the chosen") and is used of the traditional dance troupes.

Inyenzi means "cockroach" and was a derogatory word used for Tutsi during the years of ethnic hatred.

Jeunesse is the name of the bands of rebel youths in the Congolese 1964 civil war and is the French word for "youth."

Mwami is the name for the Tutsi king of Rwanda.

Muzungu (plural is *wazungu*) is a word used throughout East Africa for "a white-skinned person."

Posho is the name for the millet porridge that is made in Uganda.

Rugo is the enclosure around the old traditional Rwandese house.

Safari is Swahili for "a journey" and widely used throughout the region.

Simba is Swahili for "lion" and was used by the Congolese rebels in 1964–1965 to describe themselves.

Ugali is the name used in western Uganda for maize porridge.

Acknowledgments

My very grateful thanks go to the Right Reverend Emmanuel Musaba Kolini, bishop of Kigali diocese and archbishop of the Anglican Church of Rwanda, and his wife, Freda Mukakarinda, for sharing their stories with me. I want to thank them for their patience with all my questions and for their love and friendship since we first met in 2001.

I would also like to thank Dr. Peter Holmes and Dr. Susan Williams, who have encouraged me and helped me to write this book, and Volney James, Dana Carrington, and Bette Smyth at Authentic/Paternoster Publishing for all their work and faith in me. Without their help I doubt that this book would have ever been written.

My thanks are also due to Bishop Geoffrey Rwubusisi for sharing his story with me and to Mrs. Rose Bulamba, the archbishop's secretary, for all her help.

I am also very grateful to my dear husband, the Reverend Malcolm Millard, whose patience and love have supported and encouraged me in so many ways while I have been writing.

Notes

Introduction

1. On this day the week of mourning begins in commemoration of the Rwandan genocide of 1994.

2. Scripture Union's *Encounter with God* is a daily Bible-reading system designed to lead one to a deeper understanding about what God is saying to us and to his world today.

3. The denomination has recently changed its name from Eglise Episcopale (Episcopal Church) to Anglican Church.

4. In Anglican churches a *diocese* is an administrative territorial unit administered by a bishop; it may also be referred to as a *bishopric* or *see*, though more often the term *see* means the office held by the bishop. An important diocese is called an *archdiocese* (usually because of size, historical significance, or both), which is governed by an archbishop, who may be exempt from or have authority over the other dioceses within a wider jurisdiction, called an ecclesiastical *province*.

Chapter 1: Early Days

1. *Wazungu* is the plural form of *muzungu,* a word meaning "white person" in many Bantu languages of East, Central, and southern Africa.

2. People are buried the day they die because of the heat; so the events of the day were very hurried and confusing to young Kolini.

3. Pyrethrum was discovered to be an effective insecticide during World War I when a group of soldiers slept one night in a field where the daisies were growing. They found, much to their surprise, when they woke the next morning, all the body lice that had been infesting them had died. Rosamond Halsey Carr and Ann Howard Halsey, *Land of a Thousand Hills* (Harmondsworth, Middlesex, England: Plume Books, 2000), p. 28.

4. For a more detailed background to this issue, see Emmanuel M. Kolini and Peter R. Holmes, *Christ Walks Where Evil Reigned: Responding to the Rwandan Genocide* (Colorado Springs: Authentic, 2008), p. 33ff.

5. The White Fathers is a Roman Catholic international missionary society of priests and brothers whose sole field of activity is Africa. It was founded in North Africa in 1868 by the archbishop of Algiers, Charles Lavigerie. Their religious habit resembles the traditional clothing worn in North Africa: the white *gandoura* (a tunic) and *burnoose* (a hooded cape).

Chapter 2: Displaced in Congo

1. See Kolini and Holmes, *Christ Walks Where Evil Reigned,* p. 25ff.

Chapter 3: Escape to Uganda

1. A while ago I was privileged to attend the graduation celebration of a woman who had just gained her master's degree in nursing. She went on to hold a senior nursing position in Rwanda. At the ceremony she shared that she had attended Kolini's school at the refugee camp and had become a Christian there. Her testimony is just one of many from the students who were helped by Kolini's obedience in teaching the children and being a Christlike example in the refugee camp.

2. See details in chapter 10 and in Kolini & Holmes 2008:57ff.

Chapter 4: The Call to the Ministry

1. John's story is told in the book *The Bishop of Rwanda*, John Rucyahana and James Riordan (Nashville: Thomas Nelson, 2006).

Chapter 5: The Love Story

1. Lay readers are licensed, but not ordained, leaders within the Anglican Church. They are also called catechists in some countries.

Chapter 6: Parish Ministry in Uganda

1. The Anglican Church has services, "offices," that should be said each night and morning, read by the priest from the prayer book, regardless of whether any parishioners attend. They are the "said offices" of the church, rather like the offices observed each day in monasteries and nunneries. Although many priests do not keep the offices these days, others make it a personal discipline to recite them.

Chapter 8: Reconnaissance Trip to Congo

1. Kolini has dual nationality, both Congolese and Rwandan, but he would describe himself as a Rwandan Congolese, as the Rwandese people groups spread into all the surrounding countries. He was born in Congo but then lived in Rwanda from a very early age.

Chapter 9: Congo at Last

1. The Church Mission (or Missionary) Society is a group of evangelistic societies working with the Anglican Church and other Protestant Christians around the world. Founded in 1799 in England, CMS has attracted upward of nine thousand men and women to serve as mission partners during its two-hundred-year history.

Chapter 10: Ministry at Shaba

1. The Mothers' Union (often abbreviated MU) is a worldwide movement of Anglican women whose aim is to strengthen and preserve marriage and family life through Christianity.

2. Theological Education by Extension began in 1963 at the Evangelical Presbyterian Seminary of Guatemala, Central America. Teachers at this seminary were struggling with the question of how a single seminary could prepare ministers for a diverse range of ministry needs. They embarked on an experimental program based on the belief that the seminary would need to go to the student rather than the student coming to the seminary. The context in which the student lived began to be taken into consideration and used as a part of the training. The idea developed of decentralizing the training of ministers. The

concept spread to North America, Asia, Europe, Australia, and Africa.

3. African Evangelistic Enterprise is a Christian interdenominational, multicultural ministry of evangelism, reconciliation, leadership development training, relief, and community development. It was created in the 1960s by African Christian leaders, including Festo Kivengere. AEE leaders are African nationals who work with local church and parachurch leaders to mobilize congregations in outreach to African cities. The ultimate vision is to see an Africa of peace and justice through the spiritual renewal and transformed lives of thousands of people. Tharcisse Gatwa, *The Churches and Ethnic Ideology in the Rwandan Crises 1900–1994* (Milton Keynes: Paternoster, 2004), p. 213.

4. The Boys' Brigade was founded in Glasgow, Scotland, in 1883. Its goal is the advancement of Christ's kingdom among boys (5–22 years old) and the promotion of habits of obedience, reverence, discipline, self-respect, and all that tends toward a true Christian manliness.

5. The American Fellowship of the Brotherhood of St. Andrew is a fellowship of men whose primary mission is to spread Christ's kingdom among men and youth within the Anglican Communion. The members of the Brotherhood practice the disciplines of prayer, study, and service and meet regularly for worship, teaching, and fellowship.

Chapter 13: Background History of the Anglican Church of Rwanda

1. Ruanda Mission was the early name for the Church Mission Society branch that worked in Rwanda. It was taken from the

name of the country when Rwanda and Burundi were a joint colony of Belgium, called Ruanda-Urundi. Eventually, the name changed to the Rwanda Mission and then to Mid-Africa Ministries.

2. Shyogwe School has experienced many trials and difficulties through the years, especially during the periods of the worst ethnic conflicts in 1959 and 1994, but it has continued to teach and train young people, celebrating its diamond jubilee in 2007. Many former pupils attended the celebrations, and the day was a testimony to the work of God on Shyogwe Hill and to the excellence of the education that was provided, enabling many pupils to succeed in various professions within their country.

3. Emmanuel M. Kolini and Peter R. Holmes, *Christ Walks Where Evil Reigned: Responding to the Rwandan Genocide* (Colorado Springs: Authentic, 2008).

4. Kevin Ward, *A History of Global Anglicanism* (Cambridge University Press, 2006), p. 175.

5. Meg Guillebaud, *Rwanda: The Land God Forgot?* (Oxford: Monarch Books, 2002), p. 60.

6. Tharcisse Gatwa, *The Churches and Ethnic Ideology in the Rwandan Crises 1900–1994* (Milton Keynes: Paternoster, 2004), pp. 94–95.

7. One of the most recent achievements of Archbishop Kolini has been the building and establishment of the Anglican Theological College of Rwanda, situated just outside the capital city, at Kabuga. Now students can be trained within their own country.

8. *Journal of the Republic of Rwanda*, no. 9 (May 1991), p. 473.

Chapter 14: Archbishop of Rwanda

1. The Mothers' Union withdrew its support for a while, but the grass-roots level of Rwandan branches still continued to function and minister. Mothers' Union is a strong evangelistic movement in East Africa.

Chapter 15: Reconciliation Initiatives

1. The majority of the prisoners were Hutu men who participated in the genocide, but there were also prisoners incarcerated for other reasons, some of whom would have been Tutsi and Twa.

2. Inter-Church Aid is affiliated with the World Council of Churches. It focuses on service to refugees and church-related institutions.

3. Conference for World Peace is an African interfaith organization with offices in New York.

Chapter 16: Helping the Sick and Needy

1. Prison Fellowship International is the world's largest and most extensive criminal justice ministry. It is a global association of over one hundred national Prison Fellowship organizations. It is active in every region of the world with a network of more than 100,000 volunteers worldwide working for the spiritual, moral, social, and physical well-being of prisoners, ex-prisoners, their families, and victims of crime.

2. Mary Weeks Millard, *After Genocide—There Is Hope* (UK: Terra Nova Publications, 2007).

3. Tearfund is an acronym for The Evangelical Alliance Relief Fund. It is a Christian relief and development agency working

with a global network of local churches to help eradicate poverty.

Chapter 17: A Pastor to the North American Brethren

1. Quoted from the fact sheets of AMiA.

Bibliography

Books on Rwandan Issues

Anyidoho, Henry Kwami. *Guns over Kigali.* Kampala, Uganda: Fountain Publishers, 1998.

Bilinda, Lesley. *With What Remains.* London: Hodder & Stoughton, 2006.

Briggs, Philip and Janice Booth. *Bradt Guide to Rwanda.* Bradt Travel Guides, 2004.

Carr, Rosamond Halsey and Ann Howard Halsey. *Land of a Thousand Hills.* New York: Plume Books (Penquin Group), 2000.

Courtemanche, Gil. *A Sunday at the Pool in Kigali.* Edinburgh: Canongate, 2004.

Dallaire, Romeo. *Shake Hands with the Devil: The Failure of Humanity in Rwanda.* London: Arrow Books, 2004.

Gatwa, Tharcisse. *The Churches and Ethnic Ideology in the Rwandan Crises 1900–1994.* Milton Keynes: Paternoster, 2004.

Gourevitch, Philip. *We Wish to Inform You That Tomorrow We Will Be Killed with Our Families.* New York: Picador, 1998.

Guillebaud, Meg. *After the Locusts.* Oxford: Monarch, 2005.

_____. *Rwanda: The Land God Forgot?* Oxford: Monarch, 2002.

_____. *Service above All: The History of Shogwe as a Microcosm of the Country of Rwanda from 1946–2007.* Self-published.

Hatzfeld, Jean. *A Time for Machetes.* London: Serpent's Tail, 2003.

Ilibagiz, Immaculee. *Left to Tell.* Hay House, 2006.

Kamukama, Dixon. *Rwanda Conflict.* Kampala, Uganda: Fountain Publishers, 1997.

Keane, Fergal. *Season of Blood.* London: Penguin, 1995.

Kehrer, Brigitte. *Rwanda: Work of God, Work of Evil.* Destinee SA, 2002. www.destinee.ch

Kolini, Emmanuel M. and Peter R. Holmes, *Christ Walks Where Evil Reigned: Responding to the Rwandan Genocide.* Colorado Springs: Authentic, 2008.

Millard, Mary Weeks. *After Genocide—There Is Hope.* UK: Terra Nova Publications, 2007.

Misago, Celestin Kanimba and Thierry Mesas. *Regards sur le Rwanda.* Paris: Maison Neuve & Larose, 2003.

Oosterom, Wiljo Woodi. *Stars of Rwanda.* Amsterdam: Silent Work Foundation, 2004.

Rucyahana, John and James Riordan. *The Bishop of Rwanda.* Nashville: Thomas Nelson, 2006.

Rusimbi, John. *The Hyena's Wedding.* London: Janus, 2007.

Books with Particular Reference to Rwandan Revival

Church, J. E. *Quest for the Highest*. London: Paternoster, 1981.

Osborn, H. H. *Fire in the Hills*. UK: Highland Books, 1991.
(out of print)

Books about Ugandan Issues

Kyemba, Henry. *State of Blood*. [[?]] Corgi Books, 1977.

Sempangi, Kefa. *Reign of Terror, Reign of Love*. Tring, Herts.
UK: Aslan/Lion Regal Books, 1979.

General Book

Ward, Kevin *A History of Global Anglicanism*. Cambridge
University Press, 2006.